Anna Mateo

410·750·8967

Anna Mateo

410-750-8967

LENA HORNE

Brett Howard

MELROSE SQUARE PUBLISHING COMPANY
LOS ANGELES, CALIFORNIA

Consulting Editors for Melrose Square
Raymond Friday Locke
Christopher J. Riccella

Cover Painting: Jesse S. Santos

LENA
HORNE

MELROSE SQUARE BLACK AMERICAN SERIES

CONTENTS

CHAPTER ONE

"There was a little girl who . . .

Time: 1960
Place: The posh Luau in Beverly Hills, Calif.
Characters: White bore, black singer Lena Horne, innocent waiter, onlookers, on-the-scene reporter, Lena's white husband Lennie Hayton, guest performer Kay Thompson.

This was one of the most famous unscheduled, but not unexpected performances in the illustrious career of Lena Horne. Lena and Lennie were waiting at The Luau to have a drink with Kay Thompson, a friend and once Lena's vocal coach. For some reason Kay was delayed. Lennie rose from the table and went to the phone to call and see what had detained her. Lena was left alone at the table. They were seated at the second level of the dining room. Directly below their table, on the first level, an obnoxious white bore demanded that the waiter give him immediate service. The properly trained waiter explained that he would be with him shortly but he was in the process of serving "Miss Horne's table." The red faced, belligerent white drunk roared forth that he didn't see any reason why Lena Horne should be given any special attention;

"Hell, she's just another NIGGER!"

Lena jumped to her feet and behaved not in the manner to which she had been programmed in the early years of her career but in the manner to which she saw fit. She yelled, "Here I am, you bastard—this is the nigger you were talking about!"

Then she started throwing things—lamps, glasses, ashtrays—anything she could get her hands on. Lena was an excellent thrower. She hit the bastard—hard, real hard. The manager afterward explained: "He sure should be grateful for the bamboo—it kept him from really getting socked."

Pandemonium broke loose. Beverly Hills' *finest* were at the door. Lennie made an exit from the telephone booth and rushed to Lena's side and grabbed her. "For God's sake what happened?"

Lena had regained her "cool" and she told him briefly.

Lennie only asked, "Did you hit him?"

The waiter was leading the drunk away with blood streaming down his forehead from a cut Lena had inflicted.

Lennie was controlling her hand clutching another ashtray ready to be airborne. "You're damned right I did!" Lena answered.

"Thank God," said Lennie as he gently took the ashtray from her tense hand.

Among the interested spectators it was reported that Lena could be heard singing as she and Lennie made a polite exit! "That's why the Lady is a Tramp!"

"Why do I have to always be late for the fun?" asked Kay Thompson as she managed to push her way through the curious crowd. An on-the-spot reporter was already at the telephone calling the story into the wire services. Before Lennie and Lena had reached their home in Palm Springs the story of Lena's "bloody battle" was front page news.

Of course, as both Kay Thompson and Lennie Hayton knew, Lena had reacted as any black person would—at least any vociferous one—but apparently the entire world was surprised. What had happened to Lena? Had she blown her cool?

Certainly her behavior was quite remote from the controlled "good girl Negro image" which had been generated by a diligent staff of Hollywood press agents and performed with Academy Award perfection by Lena herself since the day she had first come to Hollywood as a "pioneer" and Walter White of the N.A.A.C.P. was writing to her and saying, "remember your position" (In other words, don't disgrace us.)

The people who thought they were reading of a "different" Lena simply did not know the real Lena. Many years before Kay Thompson had said of her, "She says what she means and she means exactly what she says."

Of course Lena had meant what she said, and had performed exactly in the manner she had intended. The same Kay Thompson, in a July, 1945 *Movieland* interview, had described Lena as "sweet, generous, modest, considerate, gentle, wise and cooperative."

Lena was all of this, but she also possessed other qualities as another interviewer observed. "She reminds one of a black panther with its strength all sheathed."

For many years, Lena kept her private life to

her family and a few intimate friends. There was too much constant pressure in public to live up to some image, especially if one was black, a celebrity and a woman.

The individual who is all of these things incorporated into one was born June 30, 1917, shortly after World War I. Her father was Edwin F. Horne and her mother, Edna. When Lena was a small child her father and mother were divorced and Lena moved with her mother from her father's home in Pittsburgh to live with her grandmother in Brooklyn.

Perhaps the real beginning of the story of Lena is to be found in an October 1919 edition of an article in *The Branch Bulletin*, a magazine of the N.A.A.C.P.

In this issue of the magazine is a grim, chubby child in a white dress and bonnet, wearing high-topped shoes and holding a disinterested rose. The caption reads: "This is a picture of one of the youngest members of the N.A.A.C.P. Her name is Lena Calhoun Horne and she lives in Brooklyn, New York. She paid the office a visit last month and seemed delighted with everything she saw, particularly the National Secretary and the telephone."

Lena Calhoun Horne came from one of the first families of Brooklyn. It was a family that never talked about the fact they were all descendants of slave women. Yet, it was the rape of slave women by their masters which accounted for their white blood, which, in turn, made them Negro Society!

Lena's grandmother was an ardent fighter for equality and a member of the N.A.A.C.P., but even she, the direct issue of a slave owner, never really knew for what she was fighting. To her it was simply an unconscious and unmentionable fact of life that it was tough to be a Negro woman. As a small child Lena sensed, but did not know, who or what the Negro woman was who stood between the two conventionally accepted extremes; the "good" quiet colored woman who scrubbed, cooked and made a respectable servant, and the whore.

Lena's childhood was a playing field—not of Eton, but of sundry visits with relatives who lived in the Deep South. Those seven lean years may not have left her with any concept of who or what she was, but with a pretty good idea of what white people were and what they thought black people were.

At sixteen years of age Lena went to work as a chorine in the famous Cotton Club in Harlem—a club owned by white "racketeers" where black performers acted for the pleasure of a solely white audience. The idea had been conceived in the brain of a white man, a writer named Carl Van Vechten, who created a best-seller, "Nigger Heaven," which capitalized on the white man of the Twenties intrigue with beautiful black women.

The Cotton Club was founded in the days of Prohibition. It was a "speakeasy" and the principal outlet for owner Owney Madden, of the infamous Madden Gang's, beer. It also served the "real stuff." "Big Frenchy" was the top henchman and a man named Herman Stark was the manager when Lena went to work there in the thirties.

The club hired the greatest black talent in America, but no black customer ever entered the doors even though it was located right smack in the heart of Harlem at One Hundred and Forty-Second Street and Lenox Avenue.

In the Cotton Club, young Lena learned to hate white men. In the South, she had been too young to see black women used as anything else but a servant. But at the Cotton Club, Lena's mother sat protectively in her dressing room every night because there was not the slightest doubt as to what the white "hoods" and the white "swells" in the club, wanted to do with Negro women.

In the Cotton Club, Lena wore three feathers in a fan dance and earned $25 a week. She wasn't thinking of being a singer or a dancer. She was just working because there weren't many places for black girls to work. She was being exploited, as were many other young black girls. Once, when Lena's stepfather complained and tried to renegotiate her contract with the white owners of the club, they pushed his head into the toilet bowl. But thank God, as Duke Ellington said many years later, Lena was jailbait.

As a young performer with images of Josephine Baker and the current headliner, Ethel Waters, dangling before Lena's beautiful, friendly eyes, Lena sensed that the white people in the audience saw nothing but her solid young flesh and its tawny color onstage. She was not ready for such exposure. She had really never lived outside the ghetto and she really didn't know anything about white people, except that some members of her family disliked them as did many of their friends and she knew she was not supposed to like them either.

Considering the conditions of the Cotton Club, this dislike was not difficult to cultivate. If Lena had to speak with one of the white owners, her speech was restricted to "Good evening, Mister Whomever" or "How do you do, Mister What's your name." She never truly conversed with them.

It was a very respected Negro orchestra leader named Noble Sissle who managed to get

Lena out of the Cotton Club and the "lifetime" contract the owners had forced her mother to sign. Lena went on tour with Noble Sissle and he treated her as a daughter, giving her the type of fatherly advice she was accustomed to. "Remember you are a lady—not a whore—don't let them treat you like one."

These words were all very well and good, but almost irrelevant to a young girl on tour who, after a night of singing, couldn't find a place to sleep or to eat even though her stomach ached with hunger and her body cried for rest. In Lena's world of recall there is the remembrance of a night spent in Indiana where, as usual, there was no place to stay and a white man—manager of a circus wintering there—who could possibly be called "a liberal," allowed the orchestra with Lena to sleep in the circus headquarters. The animals howled all night long and the stench of animal urine and feces permeated the resting place. Lena didn't really care. She didn't care if she was treated like a lady or treated like a whore. She just wanted to be treated like a human being. She had not learned to be tough, and her only thought was of escape.

Escape came in the form of marriage to a young black man her father introduced her to—Louis J. Jones.

She married a man who was the recipient of

all of the stress, of all of the cruel meaning of being a Negro in America at that time. Louis Jones had been to a black college—West Virginia State College—and he was terribly proud. But he was often refused work because of the color of his skin. When he finally got a job it was a reward for the work he and his brothers had done for the young Democrats in Pittsburgh where they lived. He was rewarded with a job as a clerk in the county coroner's office. It was tough in the thirties, very tough, but it was especially tough for a capable and sensitive black man like Louis Jones to sit by and see less capable white men getting the jobs he knew he could easily do.

And young Lena was no help at all.

Self portrait at that age and stage of her life. She had left school at sixteen to get a job as a chorine in a white man's joint, and then to go on the road singing with a band that played for white dances. She had married to get *away* from that and from the constant chaperonage of her mother.

She had not brought anything to her marriage except her youth and virginal beauty. After a day of frustration and fighting for an existence for his wife and family in a mean white man's world, Lena's husband came home to a young, dumb wife who had managed to have two children, Gail and Edward, within a very short period of time. In addition, she did not know how to cook, sew or keep house. She was certainly no prize package of a wife or mother.

Even the birthing of her first child had been a trauma which had served to intensify the gnawing hatred Lena was developing for the white man and his private world. When she started to go into labor, her doctor, a practicing black physician who had treated her during her pregnancy and had become her "rod and staff" took her to the admitting room of the hospital and then said, "I'll see you in a few days when you come home—with your baby." When Lena cried out in fear and protest, he assured her, "Don't worry. You'll be well taken care of. You're in excellent hands. Everything will be just fine."

Until that moment Lena did not know that her obstetrician—although properly licensed in Pennsylvania—could not deliver her baby in the hospital where her child was to be born. The result was her delivery was long and painful, since her fears intensified her labor pains and instead of giving birth freely and within the presence of loving and comforting hands, she was surrounded by white doctors and nurses gowned in starched white uniforms, sticking her body with needles to help release the pain and force the delivery.

It is one of the mature beliefs of Lena Horne (one shared by many eminent psychologists and sociologists) that black wives, no matter what their age or background or even their understanding of the problem, have to be terribly strong—much stronger than their white counterparts. They cannot relax, they simply cannot be loving wives waiting for the man of the house to come home. They have to be spiritual sponges, absorbing the racially inflicted hurts of their men. Yet at the same time they have to give him courage, make him know that it is worth it to go on, to go back day after day to the humiliations and discouragement of trying to make it in the white man's world for the sake of their families. It is hard enough for a poor, lower class, working white man to cope with the unbalanced economic pressures of society. It has always been a hundred times more difficult for a black man.

It isn't easy for a young woman to be both a sponge and an inspiration. Usually, the situation doesn't leave enough room for simple love. As the first physical attractions commence to wane, the youthful concept of "love" vanishes. Both young people, man and wife, become victims of a system which is all enveloping, a system which both are consciously or unconsciously trying to fight—and win. In reality, the *Rocky* dream is seldom realized.

In the case of Lena the odds were stacked against her and her husband. She was a young, beautiful, exploited black girl, who was neither smart enough, nor brave enough to struggle for too long a time to make her marriage work. And Louis Jones, no matter how much he might have loved Lena when he married her found her lacking in strengths which he needed to support his proud but frustrated ego. In the beginning, as the marriage was ripping at the seams, Lena tried to supplant the family income by singing around town for white people at their parties. Louis fantasized about "handling" her, being her manager if she returned to show business. But the possibilities of a black man putting his foot into a white-owned cabaret as the manager of a "talent" was unheard of, totally impractical. As the tensions mounted and the rift became wider, Lena knew there was one area in which she could survive—she could still sing for her supper. She might not be able to cook a supper for her husband and children or be a good hard-working domestic wife—but she could return to the only world she had ever known, the world of show business, "Whitey's World," a stage where black men and women were allowed to be players.

In 1940 Lena auditioned for Charlie Barnet

and joined his band. It meant she was not only leaving her husband but returning to her career and to the world of the hated white man. Charlie Barnet and his boys were all white, but they loved Lena and taught her that not all white men—at least not musicians—were monsters. They opened a crack in the door to let her believe that some white people could be trusted. Yet despite the basic goodness of Barnet and his boys there were endless humiliations and hurts—even physical hurts. Lena's feet "killed me" because she had spent many of her young years wearing shoes that did not fit. In the South blacks could not try on shoes before buying.

She spent a lot of waiting time in the club restrooms, when she wasn't singing because when singing with a white band, she was only allowed on the bandstand when she stood singing. No sitting of blacks was permitted.

One of the complaints about Lena was she didn't look "like a nigger." She wasn't "colored" enough and the band was often subjected, as was Lena, to embarrassing situations because the management was not aware that the beautiful, oval-faced, *cafe-au-lait* girl was indeed a black girl.

The band, for the most part, Lena admits was very good. If some restaurant wouldn't serve her, or the hotel wouldn't give her a room, the entire band just got up and walked away. Finally, the compromise was reached that Lena didn't travel with the band when it was playing "Down South."

But the world of Lena Horne was not aware of the quality which she possessed which separated her from many other striving artists. "I didn't really sing too good, and I couldn't dance, but I looked O.K." Her survival had a lot to do with black people, even though in the beginning of her career, black people gave her a lot of flack for singing with white bands and at Cafe Society Downtown.

"A survivor, honey, is exactly what I am."

Yet Lena would not have been a "survivor" if she had not been forced to. She has confessed that sometimes she has thought her "surviving" bit was pretty dumb. "I would have been better off, sometimes I think, if I could have been a whore and then just gone on home to my own bed later on. But I couldn't. I just don't believe in anything I see or hear—there's always a joker in the pack."

Lena's survival strength is both an inherited and a cultivated strength. Certainly her bed could have been a gilded one, for there is scarcely a male, black or white, who has not at some time or another been heard to utter, "Man, she could put her shoes under my bed any time, any place." She did not have to sing for her living—she had to sing for her soul and for her soul's survival.

It was when she was singing with Charlie Barnet that Lena was selected to appear in Lew Leslie's ill-fated *"Blackbirds,"* a revue which was short-lived. But during its run Lena made a record album for RCA, "Birth of the Blues."

She came to the attention of noted jazz entrepreneur John Hammond, Jr. He arranged an audition with Barney Josephson, the white owner of Cafe Society Downtown, at Sheridan Square. Josephson hired her but changed her name to Helena Horne. (This name change was short-circuited before it ever became marqueed.) Ironically, although Josephson hired Lena, he gave her hell for using *"Sleepy Time Down South"* as an audition song.

Ironically, it was in this totally white environment that Lena earned professional self-respect. It was also at this time that she discovered a different kind of "image" white people had of blacks. It was in Cafe Society Downtown that Lena personally became acquainted with some members of the white audiences. She learned that life outside the black ghetto in which she had been reared was occasionally more difficult than life inside it. She learned in order not to break under the pressures—especially as a woman—to develop a certain guile and toughness. The Lena, "hard as ice, but sometimes soft as velvet," was coming into being. She decided her survival depended upon her not letting *them*—the controlling whites—get to you, of not letting *them* see that they can hurt you. She was standing on her own threshold with her own reluctant feet. She had to choose the paths which were open to her. She soon learned that with her very special looks she could have chosen to "pass." To learn to speak Spanish. To become, with proper coaching which was easily available to her, to have cast aside her origins and in time become an international South American beauty, retreating to another continent, using a career to launch a wealthy marriage. It was being done every day.

One famous beauty, married to a Danish baron was at that very moment a ruling leader of New York and Paris society. Her Long Island home and her Paris salon were frequented by all of the famous people in the world—artists, statesmen, social leaders—and she, like Lena, had been born in a black ghetto, not far from Chauncey Street in Brooklyn where Lena had played as a small child.

Lena could have gone "overboard" in her singing by putting more spirituals and blues in her repertoire, giving herself a protective coloring. But she chose neither road. As her ego developed, she became more secure. She was determined that nobody was going to pick her "image" for her. Whatever Lena was, Lena was going to be.

She developed an isolation from the audience that was only a sophisticated cover for inner hostility. But the white audiences didn't see it. They were too preoccupied with seeing their own preconceived image of a black woman. The image Lena chose to give her audience was the image of a woman performer they could not reach.

She was too proud to let her audiences have any personal contact with her. She rarely spoke to her audience even in the small intimate room of Cafe Society Downtown. She let her audience get the singer for whom they had paid to hear, but not get the woman who remained aloof, cold as ice.

It was at this stage of her career that Lena followed one of her "hunches." Lena is a strong believer in the aspects of her astrological sign, Cancer, and somewhat superstitious. One day she awoke with a hunch to pack up herself and her small children and transport the three of them to Hollywood, although there was no reason for her to believe the movies would beckon her. In fact, she didn't go to Hollywood in search of a film career. She went on her own simple hunch and landed a singing job at the Little Troc. It was here that a Hollywood agent caught her act, called Arthur Freed and asked him to come hear this "exquisite black bird." More to get rid of the agent than to sign up a black singer, Arthur Freed agreed to come to the club, promptly at 2:30 p.m., for an audition. He stayed, mesmerized, not so much by Lena's voice, but by her exquisite physical beauty and her incredible poise for one so young. He took her and the eager-beaver agent to the offices of his boss, the mighty Louis B. Mayer.

At six-thirty, they emerged from the offices at Metro-Goldwyn-Mayer, having signed a contract which gave birth to Lena Horne, film star.

Lena had opened the lid of Pandora's box and the smoke, which was in time to envelop and almost suffocate her, curled around her slim, svelte, young bronzed body. The role she had created for herself was to be an exacting one; one in which she would become more and more introverted as she spread her lovely image deeper and deeper into the white man's extroverted wonderland.

The rules and regulations were hard core, even for white actors and actresses. They had to change their names, deny their source of origin, sometimes pose and sometimes pose as posing. What did the future hold for a ravishingly beautiful young black girl who had no intention of playing "maid" parts, or of being made-up to pass as an Egyptian or Spanish heroine? Black people were admonishing Lena, "Don't disgrace us." White people were at a loss as to what to do with this brilliant star who had suddenly fallen away from the path of the Milky Way and was casting her own light in the star-studded firmament of Hollywood Heaven.

April, 1934, the Cotton Club in Harlem, where sixteen-year-old Lena Horne had just gone to work. She wore "three fans and got paid $25 a week" and her mother sat in the dressing room every night—for protection.

CHAPTER TWO

"And when she was good, she was very very good"

The image Lena Horne created for herself was one which was and is to this day best described by the single word "unique."

It is interesting that there has never been a successful imitator of Lena Horne—although other name singers such as Judy Garland, Barbra Streisand and Ethel Merman have been expertly copied and imitated. Highly stylized actresses such as Bette Davis and Kathrine Hepburn have had their mannerisms and speech become the regular fare of popular impressionists. Sweet and low and wicked, singing in the sexy growl that can thaw the ice in a customer's drink, is Lena's own self-projected image. No one but she can do it. It is an image of a woman the audience can't reach and therefore can't hurt. "They were getting a singer, not *me*."

People who have seen her backstage before she makes an appearance have often compared her total control and poise to that of Muhammad Ali. One singer tells of going backstage and seeing Lena, beautiful of face and figure, stunningly gowned in a white satin creation which highlighted her famous pale copper skin, stalking up and down like a sleek angry tiger in a narrow space of the off-stage wing, preparing for her entrance, muttering: "I'll show them, I'll show them that I'm the *greatest,* I'm the *best,* I'm the *one* and *only* ..." Her own self-hypnosis was so contagious that her offering was what her public wanted and what she gave.

When she came to Hollywood in 1940, a great part of her self-image had been born, but it had not been fully perfected. In the early days she was "very good." She lived quietly with a relative who helped with the housework and took care of her children, although it was only Gail of whom she had full custody. (Teddy spent most of his youth with his father in Pittsburgh.) Lena had purchased a two family-home on Horn Street and had as her neighbors such film luminaries as Humphrey Bogart and his then hard-drinking wife Mayo. Lena seldom went out in public and she isolated herself from the movie colony celebrities. She enjoyed few contacts with her fellow performers, black or white.

Among her Hollywood friends at this period were Fred Finkelhoffe and his wife, Ella Logan. Her closest friend probably was Hazel Washington who had once been Rosalind Russel's personal maid and who was the mother of the famous UCLA football star, Kenny Washington.

One of her problems was her very light coloring. In attempting to concoct a make-up which would make Lena Horne look the way the studio heads thought a Negro woman should look in front of a camera, Max Factor accidentally stumbled upon his formula for his famous Egyptian pancake. The upshot was that a lot of white actresses started getting work playing Egyptians and mulattoes—roles that could have gone to black performers.

At MGM, the director always shot the scenes involving Lena so they could be cut out when the films were shown in the South. Nevertheless, the charisma of Lena Horne was of such proportions that the projection of her image on the screen dominated the films in which she appeared and her fame was growing.

In interviews arranged by the studio publicity men, very little of the real Lena Horne emerged. Her words were guarded and she spoke mostly of her deep love for music—all kinds. She confessed in one of the staged interviews with Elliot Paul, author of "The Last Time I Saw Paris," "I never knew what blues were until I got to Cafe Society. I like all kinds of music if it's good." Her own taste buds were a fermenting of jazz, blues, barrel-house, torch and just plain "corn."

The most racial statement the MGM "star" would be quoted as saying was, "Duke Ellington gets effects that no white band on earth would be likely to duplicate.

"I'm not weighing the music of one race or land or time against another. I mean that musical personalities enrich present day music with qualities that do not copy the Dixieland style which so many jazzmen contend is the beginning and the end of jazz."

So much for the thinking words of the beautiful young black star who had learned her homework and was being a "good girl," a credit to her race. None of the inner hates or the frustrations protruded through the surface of her glittering bronze skin. Yet a dual personality was formulating.

It was aided and abetted by the fact that she knew she was sharply resented by some of the working black performers in Hollywood who thought because of her light coloring she was trying to bepass her real source of origin; that in time, she would follow in the footsteps of the exotic Josephine Baker. She was criticized both openly and behind her back by black members of her profession by not giving herself a "darker" image by singing more "spirituals" more "native music." Her confrontation finally came with Ethel Waters during the making of "Cabin in the Sky," which, along with "Stormy Weather," were her only two major pictures which employed many black people. The two women became arch enemies and the story is told that once when Lena was performing before the camera and somehow was not properly synchronizing "Stormy Weather" into the microphone in the very special manner the director desired. He appealed to Cab Calloway to see if he could say something to Lena which would produce the desired results. Cab "Heigh-de-hoed" his lithe body encased in a super "zoot-suit" up to Lena and whispered into her ear. Instantly the director got exactly what he had been in search of. Later he asked Cab what in the world he had said to create such a change of rendition, of personality. Cab slyly remarked, "Two words." But he refused to divulge what the secret words were until many years later. He had merely whispered "Ethel Waters!" and Lena had become her ferocious self. How dare anyone compare her with Ethel Waters or her unique style of singing a song with a singer whose Psalm-singing style was making her whitey's self-ordained God-Mama?

Of all the blows, Lena was to suffer, certainly one of the worst must have been the one she had to endure when Ava Gardner was chosen to play the one role which should have been Lena's by birthright—the part of *Julie* in "Showboat." And to add insult to injury, the make-up used to create the mullatoe effect on Ava's beautiful face was the very Egyptian-type pancake Max Factor had developed to make Lena photograph "colored" on film. The two young women were friends and Ava felt pangs of guilt at playing the role which she knew was hand-tooled for Lena's skills as a beautiful young black actress, who was also a famous singer, while Ava couldn't sing a note! But such was Hollywood.

Each day after shooting Ava would stop by Lena's dressing room and over martinis the two girls would bemoan their fates. Ava would complain how the studio would make her listen to Lena's voice and then tell her to "Play it like Lena would." They both would become angry and let one another know where they both thought the studio could put the finished film. It was not in the conventional can.

Perhaps, Pearl Harbor and America's entrance into World War II helped indirectly to culminate the destiny which was to be Lena's so long as she was a black star in whitey's Wonderland. She had been made aware that fame and fortune would not necessarily eliminate the pains and embarrassments which were the lot of any black person in the Promised Land.

She had sent her little daughter to an expensive private school in Hollywood which specialized in teaching the children of actors and actresses. One day Gail had come home and asked Lena, "Mummy, what's a *Nigger*?" Lena went immediately and confronted the teacher, after she had attempted to soothe the trauma of the bewildered child. The teacher cooly explained that Gail would have to learn to live with the term, although it had been dropped by an unthinking schoolmate, much as a Jewish child would have to learn "Kike" or "Hebe."

Lena was livid, but she knew she was licked. She removed Gail from the "select" school and sent her to live with her aunt in the East to attend a school which was totally integrated and where she would not be the only black child, daughter of a prominent black "star." The separation was painful for both mother and child, but it probably would have been inevitable with the war scares which permeated the West Coast following Pearl Harbor.

Lena, like other young actresses, was a volunteer at the famous Hollywood Canteen, and in a very short time, she became the "black pin-up" girl for the black G.I. Joes. She was dubbed the "sepia" Hedy Lamarr. Among her friends she asked, not without studied sarcasm, "Why can't Hedy be "the *white* Lena Horne?"

Probably no incidents of social significance have affected and strained the relations between whites and blacks in the United States as wars. Commencing with the Civil War, when the black man was the focal and emotional point of serious economic and cultural differences existing in the country, exploited both by his Abolitionist "friends" and his "slave masters."

Up to the Vietnam War, the role enacted by the black man (and woman) has been both painful and disgraceful to most intelligent defenders of the so-called American way of life. In World War I the treatment of our "black troops" has been described as being nothing less than "shitty." The only saving grace came after the War when our treatment of all of the men who fought "to save the world for democracy" was almost equally "shitty." The question was born, if a man is good enough to fight for his country, doesn't he have a right to some voice in the running of said country, some right to express his opinion about his status as a "citizen," a citizen disenfranchised by his inability to vote because of a lack of education provided for him by the constitution?

By the time World War II occurred, the black man had become disenchanted but was mute. The "Promised Land" of the great industrial cities had merely substituted one type of slavery for another. The plantation with its slave quarters had been replaced by the "black ghettoes" in the large metropolitan areas which had welcomed the black man following the Civil War. Now that he was in their midst (and in many instances proving a stronger capability for survival than his equally uneducated white brother) the men in control of wealth and enterprise were in another dilemma; one which seemed to have to face up to one of the two faces on the coin—Fascism or Communism. World War II temporarily solved the dilemma. "We'll think about it tomorrow, tomorrow when a new world will be born, a world free from prejudice, hate, a world of brotherly love." The demagogue had his enemy—Adolph Hitler—and he had his panacea—"Brotherly Love."

What happened?

Lena Horne learned. She sang at army camps where white soldiers and Negroes (as they were politely called instead of "colored" or "nigger") were entertained separately. At one session for blacks at Fort Riley, Kansas, German prisoners of war got the front seats. Lena walked out.

During the war Lena and Joe Louis became two of the biggest "star" attractions at the camps. Louis, who could have obtained any officer's rank he wished, preferred to get his rank by duty served and never was advanced beyond the rank of Sergeant Louis. He wore the rank proudly because in their travel to the army camps Lena and Joe learned a great deal about protocol—and the color of skin.

Lena was awarded the honorary title of "Staff Sergeant Lena Horne of the 29th Quartermaster Truck Regiment." The citation read: "Special Order No. 21. Upon request of the Enlisted Personnel and the Commanding Officer, the following assignment and appointment in Company "F" 29th Quartermaster Truck Regiment is announced: to be honorary member and Staff Sergeant, Miss Lena Horne, 20th Century-Fox Studio, Hollywood, California."

By order of Colonel Miller.

The lighter the skin, the higher the rank of the officer. It had to be since the Army had created the officer's training school and had established an officers' corps. In view of the fact that the draft had enveloped many young blacks, a certain percentage had to be given the right to attend officer's school. Once accepted, the young blacks soon learned the lighter the skin, the quicker they were made members of the commissioned officers corps. The reasoning was the age-old logic. It was much easier to associate with a man whose skin wasn't— "You know what I mean? *Real* black— ebony." All of the cliches of racial hatred surfaced during Lena's days of singing for the "boys."

A lot of thinking was taking place in the mind of Lena Horne, "pin-up girl," "singing star," "one of the most beautiful women in the world."

What was the price of this glory?

Like a single theme it had been drilled into Lena's mind that she had to be grateful, grateful, grateful! She was made, whether she liked it or not into a symbol, and she had to be circumspect—not for reasons of personal respect, but because it was expected.

After all, she was constantly reminded that she was the first of her race to be a big "star" in the movies and she was not to step out of line, not to make a fuss. She was learning, learning that it was all a lie. The only thing that wasn't a lie was she did make money. She was "good box office." In time she began to realize that if this was not the truth, the people who were giving her such a "big break" would have dropped her like a hot potato.

Alone and contemplative, Lena began to resent what the situation over which she could exert little, if any control, was doing to her. She knew something was wrong. She knew she didn't "feel right."

She had no social life with white persons and because of her work and the environment into which she had been catapulted by virtue of her special talent, she was isolated from her own people most of the time. She was with no one. She was in limbo. Her life—however glamorous it might have appeared to the readers of the "fan" magazines—was soul-destroying, it was arid, it was neuter.

By the time the war had ended, Lena had become both a success and a rebel. At one point MGM wanted her to do a musical in which they had invested money, "St. Louis Woman." Lena refused on two grounds. She thought the script "degrading" and why should she do a show for a studio when they refused to give her a "real" part in a movie?

They "punished" her by making her tour practically every Loew's vaudeville house in the country.

Of this period she has observed that the only people she could still be herself with were musicians—white or black. "They didn't seem to care a thing about me except as a singer and as a human being." After the six to six grind at MGM Lena would go to wherever Nat Cole or Wynonie Harris was working and listen to them. Afterward they would sit around, "rap" and "jam."

And it was at this period in her life that Lena met and fell in love with the man who was to become her mentor and her husband. His name was Lennie Hayton and he was a white man and a musician.

To any biographer, the romance of Lena Horne and Lennie Hayton is one which incorporates all of the synonyms of chivalric love, unusual adventure, sexual attraction—a love affair which incorporated the ingredients of both love and hate. It is a story which, like that of *Romeo and Juliet* will be twice told, again and again with different commentaries on both the times and the individuals concerned.

A wit once observed that Shakespeare was the great playwright that he was because he had the good theatrical sense to kill off both

Romeo and Juliet and allow the audience to weep in joy and in peace, rather than attempting to imagine the *grande passion* of the young lovers surviving the daily trials and tribulations with which their families were inculcated.

The marriage of Lena Horne and Lennie Hayton survived until his death in 1971, twenty-three years.

When they met in Hollywood it was shortly after Arthur Freed had just signed Lena for MGM with the comment, "It was not the greatness of her voice, but the greatness of her own emotion while singing. When she sings about love, that's *love* and you've heard all about it."

Lennie was a composer and arranger at the studio when they met. Later he made the remark, "I never saw Sarah Bernhardt, but now that I've heard Lena, I realize I've heard and seen greatness."

Lennie had been reared in a closely knit Jewish family in New York which respected artists and musicians and fortunately had no racial prejudices. From the first moment he saw Lena, he fell in love with her and had but one desire, to be her mate in every sense of the word—as lover, husband, friend, musician-arranger. To him their union was to be the melding of mind, soul and body.

To Lena, the very presence of Lennie presented a problem that was deeply rooted in her very being. Her grandmother was the child of a Negro slave woman and her white owner, and Lena had been warned since birth that "white men will sleep with you—but never marry you." At first her attitude toward Lennie was cold and wary.

She says it was Lennie, a white man, who taught her to love. She, who could sing of it with such exquisite meaning, confesses that she had no meaning of the word until she met Lennie Hayton.

"Early in life I was without any kind of family; I was left around with people and I didn't let myself love anyone because I'd always lose them, you see. Given my experience I don't think I could have married anyone but a musician, since they had become the only people with whom I could feel I was myself."

Obviously, there were a lot of people who didn't approve of the romance. In fact, the couple were married for three years before they dared make a public announcement of the fact.

When informed of the marriage, many in her family almost stopped speaking to her. (In fact, her father did not for many years.) But Lennie's own mother and sister were, in Lena's words, "wonderful." They didn't care; their formula for happiness was basic. Lennie was an artist and Lena was an artist and together they could—and did—make "beautiful music."

For whatever Lena Horne was in the form of a "natural" talent, under Lennie's scholarship and guidance she became an object of perfection—totally and consummately unique. Lena has often called him her "Svengali."

What the critics of this "mixed" marriage failed to realize was that Lennie came into Lena's life at a time when she was beginning to feel the pressure of the self-imposed isolation of her career as well as her self discipline of being a mother. This kind of a situation is very difficult for *any* woman who is alone. With Lennie, after the marriage was announced, Lena could try to be a good wife. He was naturally able to give her the kind of support she needed from a husband. Lennie had not had to grow up under the same pressures Louis Jones had been subjected to. When they met he was an accomplished and recognized musician who had achieved considerable status in his chosen profession. He could understand her drives and ambitions, as well as her feelings of inadequacy. He could help her professionally and emotionally because he didn't have an ax to grind. He was a kind and loving human being. Lena was filled with a great deal of hate and suspicion of many people, both white and black.

When Lennie entered her life, Lena was becoming acquainted with another type of exploitation—the political kind. She spoke at meetings and rallies, not necessarily because she believed but because it was "the thing" to do. She presented the "good image." When Lennie fell in love with her she was being described in newspapers and periodicals as "a worthy ambassador of goodwill for better relations for the Negro." A talented young woman "who in addition to her beauty has brains and knows how to use them."

Lena did have brains and her brains possessed the nerve centers that recalled her meetings with Paul Robeson, who had first expressed to her an idealism which is basic to the black cause—that bitterness and anger could never win points, but pride and belief in the justness of the black cause would.

What happened to such idealistic words, what happened to Robeson, the brilliant singer-artist? Oblivion.

And what happened to his protege, the girl the director, Vincent Minelli described as a "great find," "she seems to understand intuitively what you want . . . " Her art lay in "simplicity, she permits the material to guide her and her mannerisms—except for her eloquent use of her hands and shoulders."

There she stood, five foot six and one-half inches tall, weighing one hundred and twenty-six pounds, a sepia Love Goddess, with wrist, hands, ankles, feet; slender, eloquent and expressive. What did filmdom hold for her following the war?

A farewell . . .

Cabarets offered a better scene for Lena and Lennie. If the white world wanted a delectable but unattainable *chocolate chanteuse*, Lena was available at almost prohibitive prices.

She had Lennie to guide her, to protect her.

Lena made the choice and in the eyes of a psychologist her decision would again be an element of her "survival thesis." She was disenchanted with Hollywood, with Hollywood moguls, and she knew the poison which flowed in the pens of Louella and Hedda and their ilk who were hot on the trail that she and Lennie Hayton were an "item."

They were two talented people deeply in love, confused by the world's attitude toward them and their love, yet determined to survive in love and in life. Lennie knew how to "stage" Lena for a super nightclub act with individual arrangements and good musicians to support her. He knew how to protect her and bring her into full bloom, just as one would care, protect, and exhibit a rare orchid. And Lena, herself, understood performing in a cabaret.

"In a nightclub you're you. Nothing equals the loneliness a performer feels in a cabaret. It is the most exposed kind of show business in the world. It's so physical. It's all body. There's whiskey, there's sex, there's something that's experienced only when people are drinking and having a good time in a nightclub. In a play, in a film, you are masked, you're being somebody else. In a nightclub it's you and you're at the mercy of their thoughts."

"I'm the greatest. I'm the one and only. I'm LENA!"

Lennie's hand is on the baton. She stalks with pride and authority and the lights fall on one of the most beautiful faces in the world. The thrush begins her song, the shoulder moves right to the spot exhibiting a perfect profile, and then to the left displaying the other.

Cabarets all over the world beckoned. Lena and Lennie followed. Lena followed Josephine Baker in the Borracho Club in Paris. In time she was a headliner at the Palladium in London, the Casino, the Paris Cafe des Champs Elysses.

"Europe was a great refuge for Lena," says Ralph Harris, her manager for the past thirty years. "People weren't used to a beautiful intelligent lady of black color. Over there she could walk down the street and not be stared at as some kind of a side show freak." And she could travel with a white man without creating chaos—or possibly being lynched.

Following the passing of the Fourteenth and Fifteenth Amendments, which were written to guarantee blacks protection of their civil rights, blacks were free to marry but not with whites. The laws forbidding such marriages were still in existence in many states when Lennie and Lena married.

In 1947 in Paris, Lena Horne and Lennie Hayton were officially married. They were prepared to take their stand as a couple defying convention. They were the center of a lot of "flack." Even though Hollywood accepted the fact that Lennie had been responsible to a large extent for creating the Horne look, Hollywood was not willing to accept the Lennie Haytons as a social unit. Not only was theirs a "mixed" marriage but their politics were highly questionable. McCarthyism was the name of the putrefying atmosphere which hung over the movie colony. Fine men and women of great talent were buried in the mass hysteria which had penetrated the movie industry. Metro eased Lennie out of his official role. His marriage to Lena had facilitated his dismissal.

The fact that they were interracial didn't

bother Lena, for as she explains it, Lennie never thought of her as black. He just thought of her as being someone "different," someone very special. They worked extra hard making their marriage a success because they both realized that they couldn't afford to make the usual mistakes.

Because Lennie and Lena were relatively successful, some people thought they were removed from the problems other black and Jewish people encountered. But that was not true.

After their return from abroad, they soon discovered that things hadn't improved much in America. Take, for example, the matter of housing. Lena and Lennie purchased a house in Nichols Canyon in Los Angeles and Lennie had to buy a shotgun to protect them from some of their neighbors who were signing petitions against them and threatening their lives.

In New York they found as much difficulty locating a suitable apartment as any other black or Jewish couple. The only real difference was they could afford what they wanted. They lived at the Park Sheraton Hotel for five years because they couldn't find an apartment. There were plenty around, but they were not available to them. If they were not rejected because Lena was black, they were because

Lennie was Jewish. They were once refused an apartment at the Eldorado on Central Park West, which at that time was owned by a Negro, Bishop N.C. ("Daddy") Grace. At one building there were two landlords. One was willing to rent to Lena Horne, but the other refused because her husband was Jewish.

They finally got a place through Jose Iturbi's manager. Lena ran into him in Europe in 1956. He told her Iturbi was organizing a benefit for the Rochester Symphony Orchestra and wanted her to be one of the guest performers. Lena told him she was sick and tired of helping other people when she needed help herself. She said she needed someone to give a benefit for her. Not for money, but to find a place to live. Iturbi's manager really wanted Lena to do the guest performance and so they made a deal. In lieu of payment, he gave Lena and Lennie a lease on his New York apartment.

The fifties were for them, as for other performers, years of frustration. For seven years Lena was on the "blacklist," unable to work in TV or films.

Once again her "survival" theory was put to a test. "Sure, those years hurt me financially, but they also educated me to a lot of things. I began to grow as a person under the blacklist/redlist. I didn't torture myself about it, because it's never unusual for black people to have a bad time. Unlike Jean Muir, John Garfield and the others whom it absolutely destroyed, I had a built-in alarm button. So, I could find some dimension of that situation just in being what I had been since birth, you dig?''

The McCarthy years were somewhat blunted for Lena for she was busy with her husband and their home and her children—raising them properly and sending them to school. She worked many supper clubs and her manager learned to write special clauses into her contracts with big hotels insuring her certain rights such as to come in by the front door, to be able to call for room service and to ride the elevators.

There would be no more incidents such as when she sang at the Savoy-Plaza in New York and although she was the featured artist on the hotel marquee, she was not allowed to stay overnight in one of the hotel rooms. Following each performance, Lena would enter her chauffeur-driven limousine and retreat to the famous Hotel Therese in Harlem.

She had come a long way in whitey's Wonderland and the trophy which was awarded to her came when E.P. (Yip) Harburg and Harold Arlen brought her the score to a musical they had written for the popular singer, Harry Belafonte. Harry was booked solid for several years in concerts and Arlen and Harburg decided they could re-write "Jamaica," converting the leading role, Savannah, from male to female.

Lena and the musical were the eitome of success both on Broadway and in Europe. She loved the role and imparted to it the physical body movements which were symbolic of her singing. During rehearsals and when studying for the role Lena became intrigued with "voodoo" and the powers which could be exerted when these forgotten tribal forms of witchcraft were invoked. Black became especially beautiful to her. "The blacker the berry, the sweeter the juice!"

As a performer, Lena was always totally professional. Robert Lewis, the director of "Jamaica," said she never knew a moment of fatigue, never became temperamental even when things went awry as things often do in the putting together of a musical show. No matter what happened, Lena would make her entrance (in woolen slacks and a turtle neck sweater if the theater was unheated) ready for rehearsals. Her greeting was always the same. "All right boys, whenever you're ready." And, her "boys" started up the band at the sound of her voice—hers was a command, respected and obeyed.

In whitey's Wonderland Lena was tops! She had great talent, the respect of all her peers, adoring audiences, a regal style of life which to her was natural, remarkable beauty and as Lennie Hayton's wife—she was like the wife of Caesar—"above reproach." The idle tongues of cheap gossips dared not play games with her integrity. She had done her job well, following her instructions to be a credit to her race.

She was good, very, very good, but inwardly she was not a happy person. Of course she was happy as a wife, as a mother, as a performer—but inwardly there was something gnawing at her which she knew eventually would explode. Her survival kit through the thirties, forties and fifties had been based upon the fact that she was, in actuality, an introverted personality working in an extroverted world. She had been able to create and survive within her own cocoon, but after the closing of "Jamaica" an inner movement was pulsating. When she had resided in Hollywood, she had been able to say, "I live in Hollywood, but I'm not of Hollywood." This spoken "when going Hollywood" was almost mandatory if one was to survive, was a statement of inner power and self respect which she would not deny herself.

But the "other Lena," the one nobody knew, had to come into being. Regardless of where the chips fell, Lena knew within herself

The Cotton Club was "the place" to be seen in the 1930s and until after World War II. Of course you had to be white to be a patron of the heart-of-Harlem club. Here it's New Year's Eve, 1937 and the bandleader, at right, is Cab Calloway.

CHAPTER THREE

"And when she was bad, she was . . . "

In the book, *Lena*, written with Richard Schickel, there is a cartoon by Virgil Partch which shows a drunk dancing on a nightclub table, shouting "Hey, Lena Baby, Sing Something Dirty!" She captioned it "The Story of My Life."

It was after "Jamaica" that the aridity of her early years caught up with her and she fell into an apathy based on repressed anger. W.H. Auden, the poet, has written; 'I have no gun, but I can spit."

The people who were close to Lena knew she possessed a volatile temper. She could "spit."

They knew there had been many times in nightclubs or in cabarets where her anger had reached such a pitch that she would get psysically ill and have to throw up—sometimes before, sometimes after her performance.

It was also well-known that Lena could swear—and does—spittingly or caressingly. She is one of the few members of the female sex who can throw a four-letter word into a sentence and have it come out as a compliment. But, if she so chooses, she can shove it out and leave no doubt as to her meaning.

During the early years of her career she took a "lot of bull" but she seldom exploded for the public's benefit. Her public image was so discreet that as late as 1972 *Vogue* magazine did a feature on her titled: "If They Were All Like Lena Horne!"

Even her interviewer noted that she used "ain't" for emphasis! The good little girl had seldom turned bad. In 1949 she had sued Caruso's Restaurant in Chicago for $500 damages because she was refused admission; and another time when she could not get accommodations for her musicians in the St. Louis Chase Hotel she took the matter before the Music Corporation of America with the comment: "You can fight these things all by yourself, but it seems like you've got to have help to win them."

And on February 1st, 1955 Lena cancelled her Miami Beach nightclub engagement because the Royal York Hotel refused her and her musicians hotel lodging. She stated; "Discrimination deteriorates you mentally."

She was in no way regarded as militant and was somewhat disliked by many of her fellow black performers because she did not take an active stand for black rights. Yet, silently, she always did more than she was credited with. She is a lifetime supporter of the N.A.A.C.P.; as far back as 1946 she traveled up and down California as a speaker soliciting votes for the Fair Employment Practices bill. She didn't do more until she came to grips with the black problem.

When she and Lennie were in Paris in 1960 and it was first suggested Lena write her memoirs she told Art Buchwald she was too "lackluster" in an interview. "I didn't realize it" she said, "until a fellow wrote to me and asked me if he could ghost-write my life story. He said he went to a publisher and asked him if he was interested. The publisher told him 'As far as I know, she's a dull broad and unless you can dig up some juicy scandal, I don't know what we could do with it.

The fellow wasn't discouraged 'though and said if we could come up with some sort of *gimmick* we'd have another try at it. Not until then did I realize I hadn't lived a very interesting life."

Lena searched her mind for a gimmick, but when Buchwald interviewed her she hadn't been able to come up with one. She confessed, "I hit it off pretty well with my old man. I'm on speaking terms with my mother and I've never been in a sanitarium for drinking or taking dope."

A pretty drab rap sheet for a spicey biography. Buchwald questioned her about her children. Had they suffered and ended up badly because she had devoted her life to show business?

"No," she said. "I've thought about that. Neither my son nor my daughter has run away from home. They've never been arrested either. As a matter of fact they both have completed college." (Gail graduated from Radcliffe, and Teddy was a scholarship and honor student at the University of Southern California.)

What else was there left except Lena's being mad at the world for what it had done to her?

In 1960, her attitude was; "One night one of my so-called intellectual friends came backstage at the Savoy in London to see me and said; 'What a shame! What a shame!' "

Lena asked, "What do you mean, 'what a shame?' " and he said, " 'You used to sing with so much anger, as if you hated everybody. Now you sing as if you like everybody.' So I replied, 'But that's what we fought the war for. I'm not mad at anybody.'

"Some of the lip intellectuals are mad at me because I'm not on the speak-for-my-people kick. But I discovered long ago that what I was screaming about were things I wanted for myself and my family.

"So instead of standing on street corners shouting for Negroes, I channeled my resources as a spokesman for an organization I respect, like the National Association for the Advancement of Colored People, and bow my head to Martin Luther King who's doing the job quietly and effectively down South where it really hurts.

"At this stage I can't get into any arguments as to how I've been mistreated because for the most part I've been treated pretty good. What kind of material is that for a book?"

At that period Lennie and Lena had been married for thirteen years, and they had, as she said, for the most part been pretty good years.

"About the only thing we fight about is music. He hates singers that cloud up arrangements and I hate arrangers that cloud up singers."

In 1960, Lena was pretty much at ease with

her peers—she didn't have any quarrels worth mentioning. Some people thought she was feuding with Harry Belafonte, but it wasn't true. They made a "Porgy and Bess" record together. Lena didn't like it and said it was no good. Harry liked the record and said so, but according to Lena that was just a difference in taste, in opinion. Lena was the first to point out that she wasn't much of a folk singer and that it was almost laughable to imagine her standing up in a swank nightclub in a $1,000 gown and singing "Let My People Go!"

Lena recognized the fact that many other singers were attempting to imitate her style, but she was not even mad at them. She just ignored them. "I never go to hear them. I don't want to get mixed up."

At this complacent stage of her life, her number one resentment was the burdens she had been obliged to suffer as a Negro; that of being another "first"; that she was expected to be "real nice" and a "credit to her race." By 1960, it had gotten to be a bore. "It's like when Jackie Robinson became the first Negro baseball player. He had to do everything right. He could spit on nobody because he was a first. But Ted Williams could spit on anybody he wanted to. I don't think that's fair."

In 1960 when the black problem became a dark political and emotional issue which could not be easily by-passsed, it took but a short time for Lena and the world to become aware that when she was angry, really angry, she could *spit*.

As inconceivable as it may seem, it is quite possible that Lena might never have come into an understanding of the black problem except through Lennie Hayton.

The trim gray beard worn by Lennie Hayton lent a double meaning to his qualification as an *eminence grise* of music. Lennie Hayton was a man totally without ego, an artist of quiet conviction, a husband so dedicated to the career of his lovely and brilliant wife, where he ministered as her arranger, conductor and occasional pianist, that it was more rewarding to him than if he had devoted those years to building fame, fortune and screen credits for himself.

Lennie was always a man of one distinction or another. Fresh out of high school, a Lower East Side Jewish boy, he played odd gigs in the late Twenties as a jazzman with Bix Beiderbecke, Red Nichols, Joe Venuti and Frankie Trumbauer. He graduated to a second piano chair with Paul Whiteman (Roy Bargy was on the first), then to big-time arranging and playing in the great days of radio.

At one time he was leading a band on a show for Chesterfield six nights a week. Bing Crosby was featured two nights, Ruth Etting on two and Jane Froman on the other two. In 1932 Lennie went to California with Bing, accompanied him in "The Big Broadcast" and made the arrangement for Bing's record "Please."

It was Lennie's influence that prevented the 'swing' era from being aborted. Benny Goodman had replaced Jimmy Dorsey in Lennie's radio band, playing baritone sax and clarinet. Then he left to lead a band at Billy Rose's Music Hall, but soon decided he'd never make it as a band leader and asked Lennie for his job back. Lennie advised him to wait. Not long after that Benny made it to Hollywood with his band and everything broke loose.

In 1941 Lennie joined MGM as a composer-conductor. He made many pictures, "Best Foot Forward;" "The Harvey Girls" (with Judy Garland); and "Singin' in the Rain" with Gene Kelly. He was nominated for Academy Awards for the three and was given the Oscar in 1949 for his "On the Town" score with Gene Kelly and Frank Sinatra.

After his marriage to Lena, he first took short leaves of absence to be with her, and then during the McCarthy era was given a full leave of absence. It was during this period that they made a tour of Israel in 1952. In Lennie's memory that was the most exciting moment of their lives together, both as man and wife and as internationally recognized artists. "The pioneer spirit of the country struggling to establish itself, the reaction of the audiences to Lena—well, we toured Europe ten times and nothing ever topped that experience."

Undoubtedly Lena's marriage to such a man was one of the reasons she had been able to channel and direct her frustrations about such an enormous and complex problem as the black problem, instead of exploding with impotent rage.

As the civil rights revolution of the sixties began to spread, the result was an explosion of "ethnic" pride. Suddenly the television networks "discovered" blacks. (Due to the limited forms of enjoyment offered blacks, they became the first majority owners of TV sets and buyers of articles advertised on the TV screen. It took very little time for the black economists and sociologists to take advantage of this fact and point it out to the advertising agencies and demand that the manufacturers of the products employ black actors to advertise to their "built-in" black audience.) TV screens began to frame black faces regularly as white commercial watchers learned that blacks, too, used tooth-pastes, deodorants, and cooking materials. A new sort of power was emerging, giving the nice, quiet black the freedom to be able to stand up and shout!

By 1960 most of the blacks had moved from the rural areas and now resided in urban centers, predominantly in the inner cities. Blacks had become a majority in Washington, D.C. In Atlanta, Baltimore, St. Louis, Detroit, Birmingham, Richmond and Savannah more than forty percent of the population was black. They had to be recognized and their problems had to be dealt with. The black problem was the problem of all ordinary people—but it hit the extraordinary as well.

Lena and Lennie were no exception to the rule. There were many tense moments when the couple had to stop and take stock of themselves and their emotions. Lennie's insistence that there wasn't any difference between them exasperated and annoyed Lena. She would scream, "God dammit, I am different! Some of me is and that is admirable, and maybe that's what you like about me." But Lennie's attitude was adamant. He was a genuine humanitarian and a pure musician, protected by that strange insulation musicians have. It is impossible to talk with them the way one talks to commonplace people.

Lena has written of this tormented period of her life, "All of us who had been symbols of Negro aspirations for the past couple of decades had minded our manners . . . and nothing had come of it. My generation had been sold a bill of goods . . . a cheap bill of goods."

Lena was gradually coming to realize that the bill of goods had been paid for at an enormous price. In her own instance, the price would be emotional, for as she commenced to earnestly study and become aware of the facts, a chasm was developing between her and Lennie which, in time, when she became a full-fledged political activist, would force them to live apart until both could readjust.

The educational process of finding her self-identity was as therapeutic and painful for Lena Horne as any deep psycho-analytical treatment. She was uprooting her own "roots" as she went in search of her source of origin which went far back into the pages of American history—even as recorded by the guilt-ridden white historian.

In 1619, one year before the *Mayflower* beached at Plymouth Rock, a Dutch man-of-war eased into Jamestown, Virginia, carrying twenty Africans recently pirated from a Portuguese ship's captain who was a slaver. He sold his booty into indentured servitude. Thus the first blacks to arrive in America began their new lives not as slaves but, as did countless poor whites, as indentured servants. When they worked their time out they became the

65

first free blacks, some of whom later acquired indentured servants of their own. (At least one documented black family had white indentured servants.)

But in 1711, Virginia legalized the enslavement of blacks and many other agrarian states followed suit. To make slavery stick, it was necessary to deny that blacks were human beings. The local laws dictated that slaves could neither travel nor bear arms without permission. Slaves had no standing in a court of law, and their testimony was ruled inadmissable against whites. By denying them the right to enter into contracts, even contracts of marriage, it became legal to separate husbands and wives and sell their children.

There quickly developed a hierarchy among plantation slaves, generally breaking down into three groups. Household servants received the best treatment and were the envy of the slave cabins. Next came the skilled craftsmen (coopers, blacksmiths, etc.). Those receiving the worst treatment were the slaves who worked in the fields.

By 1750, slavery seemed to be dying out, but the invention of a man named Eli Whitney, a twenty-eight-year-old school teacher who invented a machine in 1793 which permitted as much as fifty pounds of cotton seed to be separated by a single person, intervened. The efficiency of Mr. Whitney's machine gave a shot in the arm to the dying southern plantation economy and sentenced blacks to another seventy years of slavery.

Although the Fourteenth and Fifteenth Amendments were designed to protect black's civil rights, the southern states created "Jim Crow" laws which superceded the constitutional laws. Blacks were now free to travel, but not in white railroad cars. Some cities had laws which refused blacks entrance to the city without special permission. Blacks were free to marry, but not with whites. White hotels, barbershops, theaters and restaurants were all inaccessible to blacks. And to make matters worse, the Supreme Court upheld segregation as constitutional in many decisions from 1883 to 1896.

The story was never-ending. Unlike most Americans who had come in search of wealth, freedom from religious persecution, or for whatever purpose, the black man alone had come unwillingly. He had been snatched by Portuguese sailors along the 3,000 mile stretch of West Africa from modern day Senegal to Angola. Slave traders paid no attention to tribal relationships and Bantu, Mandingo, Efik, Kru and many other tribe members were thrown indiscriminately into the holds of the slave-carrying ships. Many of the slaves did not come directly to the United States but were dumped in the British West Indies for "seasoning" before coming to the mainland.

In this tangled web of racial insecurity was the heritage of Lena. Most black people knew what little they knew of their ancestry by the words and songs of their uneducated black ancestors. Tribal words and customs were perpetuated largely through the medium of music—notably "jazz."

Added to the original outrage, came the outrage created by the Civil War and the Emancipation Act when many blacks left the South and traveled North, East or West, where they did not fare much better.

Through excessive poll taxes and unfair literacy tests many blacks never visited the polls on election days. Those who did, for the most part, voted "Republican" for reasons of strategy. It was not until Franklin D. Roosevelt put some black leaders together as a "black cabinet" to advise him of black conditions, and until Eleanor Roosevelt began her championship of "Black Civil Rights," did the Democrats look to the black populace for support at the polls. And it was not until then that the germ of an idea of the need of a "Black Revolution" was planted.

It took twenty years to burst and bud just above the ground when the same Lena Horne, as a young Hollywood star, was invited to meet Eleanor Roosevelt and broke with protocol by refusing to take an orchid to the First Lady. Instead, she selected a corsage of fresh violets and yellow tearoses. It matched the blouse Mrs. Roosevelt was wearing perfectly and it was not relegated to a nearby vase, but worn proudly.

The Revolutionary Sixties were born and Lena Horne took her stand. "Despite my involvement with my own problems and despite the contentment I have found in my marriage, I find it is impossible for me to ignore the larger Negro struggle. Maybe it is because I am automatically an angry person, or maybe it is because my grandmother made me a member of the N.A.A.C.P. when I was only two years old, but basically I think it is because no Negro, whatever his situation, is able to ignore it. The struggle is becoming a revolution and I want to be a part of it in whatever role I feel best. I have only *one* condition in terms of my joining *any* fight—I intend to speak always for *myself*. I am not a *spokesman* for the Negro people nor am I a spokesman for any particular organizational branch of the fight."

In time, however, Lena became actively affiliated with C.O.R.E. and the S.N.C.C. It was in 1963, when she sang a benefit with

Frank Sinatra, that her political voice became integrated with her singing voice. Each performer was to be allowed to give the proceeds from the concert to whatever charity he or she selected. Lena chose the S.N.C.C. and set about to sell tickets by the hundreds personally to be certain that a large sum of money would be forthcoming.

At the last moment, after the programs had been printed, Lena was persuaded to include in her repertoire a version of the old Hebrew folk song "Hava Nagila." The new lyrics had been written by Betty Comden and Adolph Green; the song was retitled *"Now!"* The lyrics were not sung by Miss Horne in a sweet southern style, nor did her body move to the rhythm of the darky soft shoe. The words were highly flammable and Lena's rendition was a flaming torch of sound. The audience was frozen into silence as she sang in the real, fighting-mad, Lena Horne manner;

> "The message of this song's not subtle,
> No discussion, no rebuttal.
> We want more than just a promise
> Say good-bye to Uncle Thomas"

And Lena pleaded;

> "Just don't take it literal, mister
> No one wants to grab your sister!"

When she finished, the stunned audience as if awakened by a bolt of lightning, rose in a solid mass and cheered wildly. Many left the concert hall chanting Lena's words, "Just don't take it literal, mister . . ."

Old Blue Eyes was in a state of shock. He had been catapulted into a cause without his knowledge. His charity was some innocuous, non-political group. Lena's was the voice of the Civil Rights' Revolution.

Bud Granoff immediately produced the record for 20th Century-Fox and overnight Lena's voice was one of the voices of the revolution. She had found her role. The furor the record caused was almost unbelievable. It was destined to become a hit but it was at once banned by many stations for being too controversial—especially in Los Angeles where seven of eleven stations forbade playing the record. In New York, on the other hand, only one station was not playing the record.

Russ Barnett, the program director of KMPC Los Angeles, said; "It's pretty strong integration advocacy. KMPC would rather avoid editorializing through music." Barnett also said he didn't think the record was well-done, that "the lyrics don't fit the music."

Bob Sinn, record librarian at KNX, also Los Angeles, said, "We're not playing it primarily because we consider it controversial. We don't know whether it might offend someone. The tempo and style are kind of raucous, which we don't use normally.''

In New York City WCBS played the record just once so their listeners could hear what was causing all the controversy, and only after the announcer explained that "Now" failed to conform to a station policy against "rock and rollers;" "screamers" and "wailers."

185,000 records were sold three days after the record was released.

In New York, where Lena cut the record, she commented, "I'm flabbergasted!" That the tune was too wild a beat for the crisp-toned Lena Horne, caused her to laugh and say, "I think it's marvelous to be classified with the wailers. They are the ones who sell all the records."

Bud Granoff added, "Lena's never had a hit record and now this one—which we didn't think was commercial when we made it—is well on its way. I asked Lena to record it after I heard her sing it. It seemed to mean so much to her personally and she decided that most of the proceeds will go to the N.A.A.C.P. and to CORE."

There was a new voice of the turtle in the land, an angry voice, a voice unlike that of the girl who had been so very, very good.

Lena's decision to become actively involved

in the political revolution involved a certain kind of commitment. Lennie was the person who helped her make the final decision.

When James Baldwin, author of "The Fire Next Time," telephoned Lena in California to ask her to meet with him and other prominent members of CORE, along with Robert Kennedy, then Attorney General of the United States, Lena was not totally convinced that she could be of any kind of help (although in her own thinking she felt a personal affinity with Bobby Kennedy) and she was also aware that her commitment could not stop with her just meeting with Kennedy. She and Lennie discussed the situation.

"Shall I go?" Lena asked quietly.

Lennie answered very simply, "Go ahead. If you don't go, maybe you won't love *me* anymore."

What he was talking about was their love for each other—a good marriage based upon mutual respect. Lena might have lost respect for herself and therefore would have lost respect for him if she had made what both would have thought was a cowardly decision.

After the Kennedy meeting Lena flew to speak at a rally in Jackson, Mississippi. She was scared to death—not of the white people in the South, but of the blacks. Lena had lived in the South from time to time as a child and she could remember white policemen beating blacks on Saturday night, just for kicks.

And she could remember a lynching. She figured that the majority of whites in Mississippi had not altered a great deal, but she knew the blacks had. She knew they were a "different breed of cat" and she was afraid they might reject her. After all, who was she to give advice to people who were living a survival battle every day of their lives? She felt she would be grateful if they didn't hurl eggs at her. In her worldly travels Lena had forgotten the natural kindness and gentleness of southern blacks, of the people who had accepted Martin Luther King, Jr., with his philosophy of "non-violence" as their spiritual and revolutionary leader. Very shortly Lena learned that southern blacks didn't need "celebrities" to come to "talk" to them to "inspire" them. They knew that theirs was a People's Revolution and they had discovered their own leaders. But they treated Lena graciously. They made her forget that she was basically a northern black—a person who had been obliged to follow one pose working for the white, and wear another upon returning home.

She was working with Medgar Evers and his family and young people who were working on voter registration in a cotton patch. They didn't see Lena Horne, one of the world's most prominent black artists. They saw Lena, a black sister who had come there to help, who was one of them.

Medgar Evers was shot and killed two days after Lena visited him. It was a deed which was not to be soon forgotten—or forgiven. Certainly not by Lena.

On the night of April 4, 1968, Lena Horne, with the rest of the world, was to receive a shock which would send people reeling into a form of near insanity.

The time was 6:01 p.m. The scene was the second floor balcony of the Lorraine Motel in the black section of Memphis, Tennessee, where things had not been going well between the black and white population. The most powerful and righteous leader of black people America had ever known, Martin Luther King, Jr., (the man to whom Lena had entrusted the affairs of the black people in the South), had just finished requesting that a saxaphone player, named Ben Branch, play "Precious Lord" later that night at a meeting. The city was strangely quiet following the tumult of the preceeding weeks. Dr. King turned to reenter his room when a shot rang out sounding like the backfire of a car. The chill of the April evening had turned to frost.

The most powerful, highly educated black

men, the aides of Dr. King who were gathered in the courtyard below were startled by the sound. They looked to where their leader had been standing silhouetted in the dusk. He was gone. They rushed to his room where they found him sprawled on the floor of the balcony, blood spurting from a deep wound in his neck. Lena Horne, with a nation of angry blacks and shocked, sorrowful whites, sat for a second time in less than a decade in front of their television sets as the news of Martin Luther King, Jr.'s, death interruped every program on the air. Little did they know that almost two months later to the day, the nation would sit again in stunned silence as the news of Robert Kennedy's assassination in Los Angeles would interrupt all programming.

Lena's concept of the black problem had come a long way since 1963 when her conscience had been triggered by such pronouncements as that of Alabama Governor George Wallace: "I draw the line in the dust and toss the gauntlet before the feet of tyranny, and I say segregation now, segregation tomorrow, segregation forever!"

She had seen civil rights demonstrations in Birmingham, Alabama, which led city fathers reluctantly to desegregate public facilities— but not until the bombings of the homes of black leaders had brought on a riot. She had seen Alabama state police gas, club and whip black voting rights demonstrators as they prepared to leave Selma for the capital of Montgomery. She had seen black nationalist leader Malcolm X shot to death by followers of Black Muslim leader Elijah Muhammed as he prepared to give a speech in a Manhattan ballroom. She had seen the police and national guardsmen combat a rampage of arson and looting in the Watts ghetto of Los Angeles—an incident which ended in 34 deaths, 3,900 arrests and the destruction of more than 200 shops.

She had come to realize the meaning of Chairman Mao, leader of the Chinese Cultural Revolution's words: "A revolution is not a dinner party, or writing an essay, or painting a picture, or doing embroidery; it cannot be so refined . . . A revolution is an insurrection, an act of violence by which one class overthrows another."

The revolution of black people in the South fighting for their civil rights was a revolution Lena had described as a "People's Revolution—a pure thing, very American." She was correct in her estimation, but as time went on even she began to wonder. Had she been as naive as Alice following the White Rabbit into a mysterious Wonderland through a looking glass into a world where nothing could or would be decided?

In 1968, following the deaths of Martin Luther King, Jr., and Robert Kennedy, Lena was quoted as saying, "I don't know what to say about my hope. I guess I've almost reached the point where I've decided in my time and even in my children's time I'm not going to see much more. That's a hell of a thing to face. When people say, 'Hasn't there been progress?' I'm forced to say, 'Yes, a litttle.' But I don't like to settle for a little!"

Lena's second "girl singer" job was with the Charlie Barnett Orchestra, a "very class act." Lena was the first black woman to front the all-white band. When she left, tired of touring, she was replaced by Kay Starr, the Native American singer who, some said, "sounded a lot like Lena."

CHAPTER FOUR
"and then she became black—and beautiful!

In 1968, Lena Horne returned to Hollywood—with fame, fortune, beauty, talent, intelligence, wit and a fully developed political conscience. She returned on her own terms. Terms with the studio, terms with her family. She and Lennie had made their peace and Lena had become reconciled with her father, whom she had always adored but from whom she had been separated during the early years of her marriage to Lennie. Now her father lived with them. (They kept two California establishments—a small, rented house in Los Angeles, where Lennie and Lena's father lived together when Lena was away "making speeches" for the National Council of Negro Women, or performing in nightclubs [Lennie was again at work "free-lancing" for the studios]: the other a more elaborate home in Palm Springs.)

It had been twelve years since Lena had left Hollywood. And she had returned to make a movie with Richard Widmark.

The movie was a far cry from the early movies in which Lena had appeared, and the role she played was quite different from roles she had previously been forced to play.

"No more Tondaleo parts for me," she said, "I left because I got sick and tired of being a Negro woman leaning against a pillar and singing. I'm back because I don't have to do any of those things."

She came back to co-star with Richard Widmark ("my blue-eyed soul brother") in "Patch" playing a turn-of-the-century madam ("I run the best whorehouse in town") to Widmark's Sheriff. Not only are they in love, but they get married near the end of the film. Not one word is said about color.

She loved the part. "The clothes are beautiful. (One outfit was a long coffee and white gown with a mother-of-pearl brooch at the throat, a beaded bag to loop over her wrist, a powder blue picture hat heaped with pink cabbage roses and gold ribbon; in it Lena was a turn-of-the-century walking doll.) Considering our line of business, we've got to look better than the other women in town. There's a house in town that's second best and trying to be number one."

The plot concerns Widmark, a stubborn frontier sheriff who takes Lena, the whorehouse madam, first as his mistress and then as his wife. There is much clucking in the town of Cottonwood Springs—not because of Lena's color (which is irrelevant to the script) but because of her profession. When Lena first read the script it struck her as odd that there would be so much sin in such a small town, but she checked up on her history and discovered the town was rather tame by most standards.

In the movie Lena Horne did not sing.

When she first accepted the role, she was "scared to death" but she consulted Gail's husband, Sidney Lumet, the director, who reassured her "be simple, be still and don't act."

As Lena said, "That sounds pretty easy right? Well then, why am I pacing the floor at night, and throwing up every morning?"

The answer lay in the fact that for almost three years Lena had not been very busy in her profession. She had been deeply involved in the black movement.

"At first I wondered what right I had to run around and tell people how to do things and how to bring about change. But then I noticed that what they liked was not my speeches, but the fact that my personal determination helped theirs. That makes it worthwhile and that's why I do it. I am a black woman who is also a spokesman and it would be wrong not to be involved. I used to dream one day of retreating forever, but I know now I would have been miserable."

Retreating for Lean Horne would have meant afternoons in front of the television set, indulging her preference "for soap operas or old movies" or going to neighborhood movies "for a double bill. I'm very cheap and I insist on getting two movies for my money."

For Lena the making of "Patch" gave her the added joy of spending a good deal of time with her son, Ted. Most of Ted's early years had been spent with his father and there were certain resentments that Ted quite naturally felt against Lena and especially against Lennie. It was through the reconciliation with her father that Lena was also able to enjoy her son's company. She was very proud of Ted who lived and worked with the citizens of Watts. To a reporter, she admitted; "Ted is a potentially great man. He is honest, intelligent, and he cares a great deal. People like Ted are needed to make up for the loss of our princes. Malcolm is gone and Martin is gone, and it is up to all of us to nourish the hope they gave us.''

Lena had become outspoken; she had overcome the fear which she had also come to realize was the basic foundation for the hatred her own people had against white people.

"I was always a proud little woman before, but it was a very cold kind of thing. It was like a crutch, something I used to protect myself. Now all the young black people who have started the movement, the revolution, have released me, in a way. A lot of freedom has come to me through them, and my identity is finally clear to me. I'm a black woman and I'm not alone. I'm no longer in that symbolic world at all. I'm me, now. It doesn't sound like anything when you say it out loud, but I'm so aware of myself as a person now. I'm working. I feel. I see. And I feel good about being me. Funny.''

Lena liked playing the role in "Patch."

"I think inside me that she is black, because it gives me something to identify with. Even though I don't have to think about it that way, it gives me more empathy with her. She had to hide her hurt if she had any and she had to have great pride. It makes me feel I am very much in the world of my people.''

The twelve years had wrought many changes in the Lena Hollywood had once known—or thought it knew.

During the twelve years Lena had come to terms with herself. She could talk freely of the process of her own intellectual evolution.

"I think I know what happened to me. I finally am acknowledging my prejudices. I was always wasting a lot of time trying to like, or trying to curb my prejudices against the other race, trying to be intelligent about it.

"Now that I admit that I have prejudices and so do they, I find myself a little more at ease with people. Not liking them anymore than I would ordinarily, but not having so many hang-ups about it. I'm not afraid to feel things, even though I'm angry just as much and I dislike things just as much.

"I dislike the fact that many people don't accept the fact that we're a *racist* society. I dislike the fact that I'm still asked to side with people who think if we went a little slower, or if we didn't express our anger so, we might accomplish more. That bugs me. I guess all the cliches bother me like, "We did it, why can't you?' or 'What do you want?' It drives me up a pole."

The Widmark-Horne movie was released under the title "Death of a Gunfighter." It did not bother Lena that she was fifty-one years of age when she performed her first acting movie role in a non-segregated film. She had learned to live beyond a bitterness which could easily have engulfed her. Lena made no attempt to follow up a belated fulfillment of a career as a movie actress—without a song. She says of the experience, "It was fun, and a challenge, because I hadn't practiced the craft of acting very much. I think if I hadn't had my other life as a singer, I might have pushed ahead, but my feeling at this point was that it was too little, too late."

The late sixties and the early seventies were good years for Lena and Lennie—despite the troublesome things which were still going on around them. But these things had reached out so far as to incorporate most of the world—not just the private world of Lena and Lennie.

They were both working creatively. Lena in TV specials (three of which were produced in England; one with Dean Martin in Hollywood). Lennie, during their three year separation had taken a plunge into arranging for TV and did segments for Chrysler Theater, Voyage to the Bottom of the Sea, The Virginian, Daniel Boone, etc.

He was lured back to score another movie by 20th Century-Fox who hired him to score "Star," the film about Gertrude Lawrence. From this he was assigned to "Hello, Dolly" for which in 1970 he won the Academy Award.

Lena continued her work as an activist and

was rewarded by citations from the Urban League and a membership in Delta Sigma Theta, a black woman's social service sorority. Her children were both happily married.

Then within the span of a year or so, death claimed the three men closest to Lena—the three men who had been so influential in the molding of her life style and her character. The first to go was her father, the man from whom she had been separated as a little girl when her mother divorced him; the man she had sought out when she had gone on the road singing with a band and had found him still running his small hotel, The Belmont, a black hostelry in Pittsburgh in which her father had a gambling room named "The Bucket of Blood;" the man who knew the street and street people; the man who introduced her to her first husband, Louis Jones; the man who had refused to speak to her for years after her marriage to Lennie Hayton, a white man; the man who came to spend his last days with Lena and Lennie; the man who, when he was dying, Lena brought fresh lobster as a "last supper;" the man who, Lena said, through her tears, "instilled in me from the beginning a willingness to accept the fact that some of the great things just couldn't happen for me. Everything inside me that was like him has protected me."

The flowers had scarcely withered on the grave of Edwin Horne when twenty-nine-year-old, Teddy—he who had the true "potentials of greatness" died of a kidney infection.

Teddy had become close to Lena in the last years, in the years when she came to an understanding of herself and her role in the black revolution of which he was a part. It was Teddy who opened up to Lena his world—a world of being young, of being wise, of being black.

And finally Lennie. Lennie who had been her rock, her foundation, her solace, a gently flowing fountain of knowledge; Lennie who had made her strong and cognizant of the fundamental truths of life and love.

The trio had loved Lena and had fortified her with much of their strengths. "I was very lucky to have three men who taught me so very much, who left me with the courage to carry on—even when they were no longer with me."

The triple blow was almost too intense for Lena. She was at a loss to describe how she felt. She was concerned that she did not immediately have the big reaction, the complete breakdown, and she lived in fear that it might occur. She resolved not to think about it. Not to destroy herself with another fear, to keep herself occupied.

And so she stepped into the busiest period of

her long career. She was fifty-seven years of age, still trim and exquisite.

She was now an incomparable product of a black middle class, who grew up as a black bourgeoise, and who was reaping the greatest joy of her life in the respect she had gained among the young, particularly the young blacks who had to struggle much harder than she—people from whom, during her escapist years, she felt alienated.

"There's a group of girls—Dionne Warwick, Lola Falana, Mary Wilson, others—who call themselves Bravo. When I opened with Billy Eckstine at the Circle Star Theater in the Bay Area, they came to see me and gave me the most beautiful ring. They said I had been a sort of mother figure who had made them all possible. To me, that was a tangible assertion that I am Lena Horne—a persom—something I can put my finger on; if I can coin a word, let's say I'm part of a generativity of my own young people.

"They said, 'While you're still alive we want you to know this.' They knew all about the dues we paid back then. Well, that's the kind of marvelous thing that happens, coming from my peers and young ones.

"Hell, the Urban League can give me all the citations in the world, but when I see Aretha Franklin and we put our arms around each other, I really feel I'm part of the whole thing. I never did before.''

If Lena still had any doubts about her "being a part of it" they were banished in 1974 on a concert tour with Tony Bennett. The ominously commanding figure of the highly polished Miss Lena Horne made a crucial decision. "The stoning of black children and the beating of black citizens forces me to cancel my appearance." The city was Boston, that same city where the Abolitionist movement had recieved its greatest support, a city where the black man at the time of the Civil War sought and had been given refuge, a city which was the cradle of the American Revolution.

Tony Bennett agreed and cooperated with Lena. "It cost thousands of dollars," she said. "But it was worth it."

It proved to the world where Lena Horne, the girl of French Sengalese, Blackfoot Indian and white descent stood in a world still confused by racial prejudices. The girl "who didn't sing colored enough" had taken a proud and courageous stand, a conclusive stand on behalf of her source of origin. She was totally black—and more beautiful than ever.

In 1978 Lena Horne returned to the stage in the female lead in a revision of Cole Porter's "Pal Joey" titled, "Pal Joey '78."

The project was the fruition of a deal which had been pending for years. First, Lena was approached to do it as a 90 minute TV special with Sammy Davis Jr., but the deal fell through. Then Gene Kelly (the show's original 'Joey') came to Vegas to see Lena about to do a revival. Lena agreed provided they could get a Joey of the calibre of Ben Vereen. (The play is actually not about Vera, the role Lena was chosen for, but about Joey, the heel.) The producers finally settled on Clifton Davis. The producers obtained permission to interpolate a few extra songs for Lena, among them "A Lady Must Live" from "America's Sweetheart" a 1931 show, and "This Can't Be Love" from "The Boys From Syracuse" vintage 1938.

Being in the play was like old home week for Lena. Josephine Premice, who played Melba, Vera's girl friend, had played in "Jamaica" twenty-one years before. Claude Thompson, who had been in the chorus of "Jamaica" was the choreographer. John Myles, who was the musical director for Lena's first big TV special for Monsanto, was the conductor. And Michael Kidd, who came in to replace Gower Champion, had been one of the neighbors and friends of Lena and Lennie when they had lived in Nichols Canyon and had helped to squelch the other neighbor's unfriendly attitude toward the couple.

The role Lena Horne played was written for Vivienne Segal originally and Miss Segal came out of retirement to again play the famous role with Harold Lang dancing Joey. To enact a role which most critics felt belonged totally to Vivienne Segal presented quite a challenge to Lena, but amazingly she found it easy to assimilate.

"I discovered that a great deal of my own life was useful in portraying her. It's tongue-in-cheek, of course, but the Vera part says something of how old women, middle-aged women, who are romantic at heart, play these little games with themselves. It's quite logical that somebody younger is going to need them. I find the play very real, very believable."

Unfortunately the critics did not cotton to the revised edition, but the popularity of Lena was so great that the play was solidly booked for more than a year. (In the author's circle of Horne admirers she knows one individual who saw sixteen performances.) The musical version may not have been John O'Hara's story, nor pure Cole Porter, but it was a showpiece for Lena, and her vast circle of admirers kept the box-office receipts flowing. The one thing "Pal Joey" did accomplish for Lena's reputation was that it provided that basically she could always have been what she had once again become in the show—an accomplished actress whose multiple gifts include all the qualifications for musical comedy. But because of her color her entire movie career consisted of two early, naive, Hollywood style, all-black musicals followed by a series of cameo vocal appearances in which she had no acting parts. Not until "Death of a Gunfighter" with Richard Widmark in 1969 was she accorded a serious acting role in a major motion picture.

As a warm-up for her role of Vera, Lena accepted a role in the movie, "The Wiz," directed by Sidney Lumet. The irony was that Lena was working for her son-in-law, while his marriage to Lena's daughter, Gail, was floundering. Lena had always been very close to Gail and through the years had become quite fond of Lumet.

"Sidney's a workacholic. I think he's just brilliant. In the beginning I didn't want him to marry Gail, but after a while I grew to be his Jewish mother. They were married quite a while. (Lena's granddaughters Amy was thirteen and Jennie eleven when the Lumet marriage was dissolved in 1978. The Lumets had married in 1963.) I guess I took it harder than anyone as mothers usually do and it left me in a state of shock. I tried to keep out of it. I realize its selfish on my part to want everything to be like a fairy tale."

Since Lennie's death, Lena had sold their home in Palm Springs and she had lived for several years on Manhattan's Upper East Side, a few minutes walk from the Lumets. The divorce was another rift in Lena's own personal life style. She determined to leave Manhattan and take up once again a permanent residence on the West Coast. She found the house of her dreams in Santa Barbara.

"I thought I'd never be able to leave Manhattan (for years following Lennie's death, she swore she'd never own another home of her own) but I became tired of seeing those poor ladies with their brown paper bags lugging their possessions from street to street. I became miserable about misery. Something inside said, 'Help! Get me out of here.' "

Ironically nobody but a housekeeper was to see the house because of "Pal Joey" bookings and the making of "The Wiz."

In "The Wiz" Lumet assigned Lena the part of Glinda, the good witch. Remembering how the audiences had for years relished Margaret Hamilton in the original "Wizard of Oz" as the *wicked witch*, this was the role Lena coveted. She said to Sidney, "You know I don't like to sing those sweetie-pie inspirational songs." But Lumet just laughed and told her "You're stuck with that image and there's nothing I or you can do about it."

Then Lena got to listening to the song, "If you Believe" and it became "an anthem for me and I loved it." In her words, "It symbolizes the whole plot." Then with the wonderful Horne impish grin and sultry growl she confesses, "Anyhow, I didn't sing it all that sweet!"

Lena Horne is alternately gregarious and a loner. "I'm really happy when I'm either alone or with a group of people I feel very close to. I enjoy making my associations into a circle that becomes my family." It became like that with the "Pal Joey" company. The lonely gap caused by deaths and divorce in her own personal family was temporarily filled and to her public these tragedies apparently worked no detectable hardships either on her timeless physical beauty or her resilient inner strength.

"I enjoy the exchange of ideas between the generations. The dancers and singers all send off such great vibrations of talent; we understand one another and love it."

Lena's image varies according to the age, race and attitudes of the observer. To many young blacks she is a symbol of triumph over bigotry and segregation that pervaded show business in the forties. To some she is no less significant as a survivor who outlasted political repression during the McCarthy era when she was kept away from movies and television for seven long, lean years.

However, most admirers think of Lena primarily as a singer and that is an identity she wears with grace, growing confidence that was always under-estimated because of the pre-occupation with her fantastic beauty. An early product of musical show business she grew to understand music more fully during the two decades as Lennie Hayton, the composer's wife. But to the very day of this writing Lena Horne finds nothing more exhilarating than a tour with a band. She loves it.

"I always feel the band is my life, my family. When I went on tour with Count Basie for five whole weeks, the show got incredible reviews. It was fantastic to go out onstage and sing with my band booting me right in my rear end and Basie would say, "Hello, Pretty Girl," the same as he had always done."

Lena Horne, the sexagenarian, was summing up the career of Lena Horne. Fate, which had played many strange tricks upon her, had chosen the latter years to bless her—to create Lena, the Horne of Plenty.

It was epitomized on the night of her sixtieth birthday when she was on the road with Vic Damone and having a ball! They were in New Orleans and the town celebrated Lena Horne's birthday as only the town of New Orleans could. The mayor came and gave her the key to the city. "It was beautiful. They rolled out a huge cake as big as a dining table and at midnight everyone started singing 'Happy Birthday' and everyone was crying. It was quite special. In fact, there was such a big to do going on, I said to myself, Lord, maybe this is the last year!"

But it wasn't. It was only another beginning of another decade in the remarkable career of the remarkable Lena Horne, the girl who didn't look or sing colored, but became black and beautiful to the entire world.

The "most important man in Lena Horne's life" was bandleader Lennie Hayton seated at the piano with his band. An extremely talented man who arranged, conducted and composed, and, uncompromisingly loved Lena Horne. She, in turn, has said, "I never knew what love meant until I met Lennie."

Lena Horne was signed by MGM as a contract player in 1942 but the studio really didn't know what to do with her. For the next two years they cast her singing in musical sequences but never gave her a role of substance—nor one that couldn't be cut out of the film if a theater owner objected to her race!

In the 1940s every pretty woman put under contract to a Hollywood studio was required to pose for provocative "pin ups" and Lena was no exception. While the musical appearences did little for her career, the pin ups made her popular with World War II GI's and the fan mail poured in!

CHAPTER FIVE
Music is My Lover
(The Big Bands)

If as Duke Ellington claimed in his auto-biography "Music is My Mistress" then a biographer of Lena Horne is quite within reason to say of the lady that music is her lover, is her life.

From the day she went with her mother for an audition at the famed Cotton Club, the story of Lena Horne is a point-counterpoint story of American music for at least one half century. It was a half century that saw many changes in musical forms, in types of musicians.

It saw music become one of America's biggest industries and it saw people of talent overnight become millionaires, leaders of fashion and spokesmen for political beliefs. From the night she first set foot, at the age of sixteen, on the stage of The Cotton Club, the name Lena Horne and the woman were totally integrated in the movement and in the industry of music.

Although Lena's personal recollections of the Cotton Club are not too pleasant, from the wider point of view of musicians such as Duke Ellington and from audiences who gathered there, the Cotton Club was regarded as a classy spot. Impeccable behavior was demanded in the room while the show was on. If someone was talking loud while Letitia Hill, for example, was singing, the waiter would come and touch him on the shoulder. If that didn't do it, the captain would come over and admonish him politely. Then the headwaiter would remind him that he had been cautioned. After that, if the loud talker still continued, somebody would come and throw him out!

The club was upstairs on the second floor of the northeast corner of One-Hundred and Forty-Second Street and Lenox Avenue. Underneath it was what originally was the Douglas Theatre, which later became Golden Gate Ballroom. The upstairs room had been planned as a dance hall, but for a time the former heavyweight champion Jack Johnson had run it as the Club De Luxe. It was what was known as a big cabaret in the days of the twenties and the thirties, and it could seat four to five hundred people. Lew Lewis was in charge of producing the shows and until 1927 a house band was led by Andy Preer.

Sunday night was the big night in the Cotton Club. All the biggest stars in Manhattan, no matter where they were playing, showed up to take bows.

After Lew Lewis, Dan Healy staged the shows and on Sunday night he would introduce the stars. Duke Ellington was the leader of the house band and somebody like Sophie Tucker would stand up and the Duke would play her song, "Some of These Days" as she made her way up to the stage to take a bow. It was all done in a pretty grand manner.

Harlem had a tremendous reputation in the twenties and thirties, and it was a very colorful place. In the early days of the Dutch settlement of New York, the area had been the site of huge farms and many handsome town houses, selected for their propitious views overlooking the Hudson River where the great boats sailed upstate toward the Canadian border via Albany and Buffalo. The site commanded a full vista of the area which set it apart from Manhattan—Central Park. Harlem stretched from the Hudson to the East River and following World War I it became an attraction in Manhattan, like Chinatown in San Francisco or the French Quarter in New Orleans. "When you go to New York," people said, "you mustn't miss going to Harlem!" And in Harlem, the Cotton Club was the top place to go.

While the chorines such as Lena were not paid large salaries, the headliners were, and the customers paid high prices for the entertainment, the food and the drink. The girls in the chorus were without doubt the most beautiful "black" beauties to be found. The chorines in the Cotton Club chorus were comparable to the Zeigfeld Follies beauties, the Earl Carroll dolls and Billy Rose's long-stemmed "roses." There were about twelve dancing girls and eight show girls and they were all gorgeous and delectable. The girls wore elegant frocks and furs and on Sunday nights, when celebrities filled the club, the girls would vacate the dressing rooms after the show and appear in all their finery. Everytime they went by, the stars and the rich people would be heard saying, "*My*, who is that?"

It was the inspiration for Duke Ellington's "Black and Tan Fantasy." Even though Lena was "jailbait" when she danced there and was too thoroughly chaperoned by her ever-anxious mother to be a real part of the glamour, it was in this setting that Lena fell in love with music and musicians and it was from this "black and tan" fantasy that she escaped during her brief early marriage.

The influence of the Cotton Club and the friendship of the Duke were to be integral parts of the whole Lena Horne. Ellington's "flair," in addition to his musical genius, intrigued Lena and she retained in her mind his appreciation for "witchiness" in women. She never forgot his words: "The saddest thing—a woman who once was a "*witch*" and thinks she still is—but isn't."

Lena determined such a fate would not befall her—and it hasn't. Nelson Algren once observed, "If society denies someone their reality, then they'll structure their own reality." These words are especially appropriate for both Lena Horne and Duke Ellington, whose brilliant careers are interwoven in the tapestry of black American music. Lena, who never really had great confidence in her own talent, gave herself a protective coloring of icy aloofness. The Duke, on the other hand, from his adolescence never had any qualms about his musical talents, yet, he remained an enigmatic, elusive man who never in his life completely opened up. The "love you madly" facade—just the opposite of Lena's "look, listen but don't touch"—the grandiloquent speeches to his audiences, the sardonic humor, all covered emotions he was never willing to expose.

The structuring of the careers of the two talented musical figures is to be found within the history of one of the musical phenomena of the century—the Big Band.

Noble Sissle led one of the first Negro orchestras to be featured in white night clubs, one that specialized in playing for floor shows. Sissle was a well-schooled musician in the early twenties who had written the score for a very successful show called "Shufflin' Along." His band seldom projected much musical excitement, though from time to time it featured such diverse jazz soloists as Sidney Bechet and Charlie Parker and in 1937 it spotted a young singer named Lena Horne and removed her from the Cotton Club to the bandstand as a vocalist. What Sissle seemed to want to do more than anything else was to repudiate the stereotype of the Negro musician by showing he could play something other than jazz—and to introduce a black girl singer who was radiantly and exotically beautiful by any physical standards. He succeeded eminently in doing both. He gave Lena her original lacquer of "class."

In 1941, Charlie Barnet signed up Lena Horne who recorded four tunes with the band, the most notable of which was "Good-fo' Nothing', Joe." Bob Carroll, the robust baritone who sang with the Barnet band at the time, recalled the first day Lena appeared. "We were working at the Windsor theater in the Bronx and something happened to the girl we were using. Somebody remembered the pretty girl who was working in the movie house and they sent for her.

"It was Lena. I remember the long, straggly hair and that her dress was not particularly attractive. She ran down a few tunes in the basement of the theater, and then, without any arrangements, she did the next show—not only did it, but stopped it cold. She was just great!"

It was his own talent for discovering such new fresh talent that made Charlie Barnet the great band leader he was. Charlie, a friend of the author, still, in an interview at 81 years of age, had vivid recollections of his band days.

"The band business was a romping, stomping thing, and everybody was swinging, and I can't help but think back to the group of boys in the band. It was a happy band, and even with the one nighters it was a ball!"

For Charlie Barnet and the many fine musicians who played in his ever-swinging outfit, and for the pretty girl singer, Lena Horne, the big band days must have indeed been a ball.

Charlie was the kind of a guy who believed in a good time—not only for himself but for all of those around him. He and his cohorts projected a happy, carefree, swinging feeling both in their music and very often in their attitude toward life. They were disciplined in their playing, for Charlie always respected music, and they took their task seriously. But themselves—no! This was a band that reflected the wonderful ad-lib spontaneity that characterizes jazz. Its music always had a beat. And like its leader and his many sidemen it was always colorful.

Barnet was a Hollywood handsome-hero sort of a man—in fact, at one time he tried making it as a movie actor, appearing in two films—"Irene and Mary" and "Love and Hisses." But his heart wasn't in acting and he was always faithful to music.

As a kid he rotated toward jazz. His family wanted him to study piano. He wanted to play drums and he commenced beating on his mother's hat-boxes, sundry pots and pans and lots of expensive paraphernalia—for he was from a very wealthy family.

His mother's father, Charles Daly, had been the first president of the New York Central Railroad, and Charlie's parents had all manner of "respectable plans" for their son. They sent him to Rumsey Hall and Blair Academy and he was enrolled at Yale. But this was not meant for Charlie. By the time he should have been preparing for his freshman mid-terms at Yale he was in the South, blowing his wild tenor sax in any of the sundry outfits who would allow him.

Barnet's style was greatly influenced by Coleman Hawkins. When Charlie was twelve, his family gave him a C-melody sax which was a cross between an alto and a tenor. He learned to play "hot" by playing the Victrola. He was "nuts" about Fletcher Henderson and when he heard Hawkins he switched to the tenor. When he heard Johnny Hodges of Duke Ellington's band play alto and soprano sax he switched to those horns, too.

Ellington's band had a big effect on Barnet's band, and when after having fronted a fairly commercial outfit for several years, Charlie decided to cash in on the big-swing band craze, he patterned his arrangements after the Duke's. An article in *Metronome* called Charlie Barnet's band "Barnet's—the Blackest White Band of All!" So dedicated was Barnet to the Duke that, when he built a fallout shelter after the war, he stocked it with a superb collection of Ellington recordings.

When he first founded his band, he had such noted musicians as Harry James and Ziggy Ellman. Before he had Lena for a girl singer he had Harry von Zell, who later became a famous radio announcer.

Charlie himself sang, and sang well. His voice was rather nasal, but he had a good beat and a good sense of phrasing. He featured his tenor sax a great deal—an exciting, booting, extremely exacting rythmic horn. He could also play soulfully. Two recordings made with Red Norvo, "I Surrender, Dear" and "The Night is Blue" are highly recommended not only for Barnet and Norvo but for three then non-recording artists; clarinetist Artie Shaw; pianist, Teddy Wilson; and trombonist Jack Jenney.

Barnet liked to surround himself with aspiring musicians. And he especially liked black musicians who were aspiring. It could well have been because of his liberal attitude on the racial question (especially liberal for his time) that his band was never picked for any radio commercial series featuring big bands.

He even had some trouble procuring engagements in many sections because of his attitude. But he refused to compromise. It was a factor which endeared him to Lena and a factor which made the first step for her understanding of the white musician and her acceptance of him as an equal.

It is interesting to note that when Lena left the band she was replaced by another newcomer, Kay Starr, a white girl vocalist who has been credited as being the only white girl singer who could sing like a black.

The music of the big bands varied from band to band, from style to style. In the era of the big bands you could hear all kinds of swing bands: the hard-driving swing of Benny Goodman; the relaxed swing of Jimmie Lunceford; the forceful Dixieland of Bob Crosby; the simple riff-raff swing of Count Basie; the highly developed swing of Duke Ellington; and the very commercial swing of Glenn Miller.

Many of the big bands were built around the leaders and their instruments, the clarinets of Artie Shaw and Benny Goodman, the trumpets of Harry James and Bunny Berigan, the trombones of Jack Teagarden and Tommy Dorsey, the tenor sax of Charlie Barnet, the pianos of Ellington and Basie and the drums of Gene Krupa.

And then there were the singers—the band vocalists as they were called. Many times they played important roles in establishing a band's popularity, in some cases even surpassing the band itself. Such stars as Frank Sinatra and Jo Stafford bring back memories of Tommy Dorsey, Doris Day of Les Brown, Ella Fitzgerald of Chick Webb, Peggy Lee of Benny Goodman, Lena Horne of Charlie Barnet.

But of all the factors involved in the success

of a dance band—the business affairs, the musical style, the arrangers, the sidemen and the vocalists—nothing equalled in importance the part played by the leaders themselves. For in each band, it was the leader who assumed the most vital and the most responsible role. Around him revolved the music, the musicians, the vocalists, the arrangers and the commercial factors involved in running a band, and it was up to him to take these component parts and with them achieve success, mediocrity or failure.

Of these leaders it could be said some were completely devoted to music, some to the money it could bring.

Some possessed great musical talent, some possessed none.

Some really loved people, others merely used them.

Some were extremely daring, others were stodgily conservative.

Some were motivated by their emotions, others by carefully calculated courses of action.

And for some, leading a band was primarily an art; for others it was basically a science.

The big band days were exciting and rewarding for the top musicians. For them there was glory, there was glamor and there was good money. For them it could be a thrilling ball, a

Cinderella dream come true. For others it could be a chilling bore, a nightmare come much too true. It was a good life for the star soloists and for many of the lead musicians. Tommy Dorsey once compared a dance band to a football team. In the backfield he put the soloists—the obvious stars. And in the line he put the lead men—the first trumpet, the first sax and first trombone, along with four men in his rhythm section—the pianist, the guitarist, the bassist and the drummer.

But there were many other musicians, those who played in sections but didn't lead them. The morale of these musicians were generally highest in the bands that played the best music and were headed by leaders who knew not only how to treat their music but the men who played it. Life in general was most rewarding to the musicians in big bands who were being paid—well paid—for doing something they would have chosen to do even without pay. There were numerous minuses though.

The actual living conditions of most musicians would have been pretty difficult to take if they hadn't had their love of music to sustain them. The numerous one-night stands could be pretty discouraging. Planes and trains were too expensive and impractical (in some instances Jim Crow laws prevailed and the bands were separated in travel) so traveling was confined almost exclusively to chartered buses or private cars, none of which offered the riding ease or luxuries of today's vehicles. Many times bands would arrive at ballrooms or a dance pavillion by bus, wash up, change clothes in a dingy dressing room or washroom, play the job, hang around waiting for something to eat, climb back on the bus and try to grab some sleep enroute to the next stop. Some of the one night jumps were pretty frightening, especially in winters and in mountainous areas. Accidents took their toll. Hal Kemp was killed in one. Charlie Barnet lost two top musicians in another.

Obviously though, they were all part of something more inspiring than mere materialism or fleeting fame. They shared what too few working groups do—a love of what they were doing, a love coupled with a healthy conviction that they were both playing and fighting for a cause to which they were deeply dedicated. In addition, most musicians were guarded by the protection of their peculiar insulation system. Jazz musicians especially, possessed their own brand of humor, the kind that led them not only to laugh at humorous events which concerned others but themselves also. Unlike many others, most jazz musicians have possessed the happy faculty of not taking themselves too seriously. Their work yes, themselves, no.

As for the vocalists, how important were they really to the big bands? Very. Some hipper jazz-oriented fans and musicians have resented them, but in the over-all picture, it was the singers who provided the most personal, the most literal and often the most communicative link between the bandstands and the dance floors, between the stages and the seats, and between recording and radio stations and the perennial "unseen audiences."

What was the role of a girl singer like Lena Horne? Being on the road with a group of guys is not easy. There was no crying at night, no missing mama or running home. But it developed that inner strength that is so characteristic of Lena Horne. As a girl vocalist, she had to discipline herself musically in every way. She learned how to work in front of people and to deal with them. Band singing taught all of the fine girl singers the importance of interplay with musicians. Lena and the others had to learn to work close to the arrangement. Even if the interpretation of a certain song wasn't exactly what she wanted, she had to make the most of it. Like Peggy Lee, Lena concedes, "I learned more about music from the men I worked with in bands than I learned anywhere else. They taught me discipline, and the value of rehearsing and how to train."

Lena once heard Frank Sinatra observe that he learned much of his phraseology just sitting on the bandstand watching Tommy Dorsey blow his trombone. Because of his breath control, Sinatra pointed out, "Tommy could make it all sound so musical that you never lost the thread of the message."

So impressed was Frank with Tommy's physical prowess that he began taking extra breathing and physical fitness exercises and a series of under-water sessions in the hope that he would learn to breathe as effortlessly as his leader.

The star vocalists all agree that in order to become a star vocalist, "get a job with a band and sing, sing, sing. There's no teacher like experience."

With girl singers, naturally, the physical factors were more demanding than with the males. Good looks, good grooming, a good figure, attractive dresses and poise were almost as vital as talent itself. And a built-in ability to deal with all kinds of people.

A single girl among a group of men certainly has a pack of troubles to begin with. If her leader was especially wolf-bent, and many of the band leaders were, the difficulties increased in proportion to the leader's demands and his ardor. And then there were the musicians in the band itself.

Lena and the other girl singers had to be tactful in dealing with the group as a whole in a day-to-day relationship. Some girls tried hard to be one of the boys (one soloist, Anita O'Day, went so far as to dress in a garb similar to that worn by the men in the orchestra), an attitude which was often resented. Some, like Lena, protected themselves with a pronounced air of independence. Still others tried the extra-feminine approach, which sometimes resulted in the capture of one man for good.

Many of the girl singers ended up marrying guys in the band. Peggy Lee married Benny Goodman's guitarist, Dave Barbour; Jo Stafford married Tommy Dorsey arranger Paul Weston; Kitty Kallen married Jack Teagarden's clarinetist, Clint Garvi—just to mention a few. Some of the girls married their bosses. Harriet Hilliard to Ozzie Nelson; Georgia Carroll to Kaye Kaiser; Dorothy Collins to Raymond Scott Trotter; Ann Richards to Stan Kenton. And, of course, Lena Horne married Lennie Hayton, arranger, bandleader and boss.

Sometimes a girl singer would do so well with a band that they became as familiar and as important to the public as the band itself. And when the musicians union called a lengthy and defeating strike in the early Forties, a number of the vocalists whose debut and development had occurred in those bands began to take the play away from them.

When the big bands began to fade in the mid-Forties it was the vocalists—especially those with the most talent and brains—who emerged as big stars. Among the men were Sinatra, Perry Como, Dick Haymes, Billy Eckstine, and Vaughan Monroe, along with Count Basie's Joe Williams, Freddy Martin's Merv Griffin, Kaye Kaiser's Mike Douglas and Glenn Miller's Johnny Desmond. Among the girls were Peggy Lee and Doris Day, Harry James' Helen Forrest, Earl Hine's Sarah Vaughn, Lionel Hampton's Dinah Washington and Charlie Barnet's Lena Horne. That's a mere handful of an enormous list of big band graduates.

What is the most interesting factor to a student of this era of music is the fact that in the years immediately following the big band era and preceding that of the rock and rollers (roughly from 1947 to 1953) just about every top pop singer with the exception of Nat King Cole, Dinah Shore and Kate Smith had come out of big bands. Even Bing Crosby, firmly established as the world's foremost singer by the time the big bands had begun to take over in 1935, had already received his musical experience and education, and had paid his dues, in the bands of Paul Whiteman and Gus Arnheim.

So the vocalists might have done a lot for the big bands—but it was nothing in comparison for what the big bands accomplished for them. And Lena Horne is one girl singer who has never forgotten. In the latter years, when she has chosen to do concert work, she has made many "concert" appearances as guest soloist with some of the big bands who have survived—notably Count Basie, who was one of her favorite musicians.

The Count was and is a musical legend unto himself, like Duke Ellington and Louis Armstrong. Earl Wilson once asked where Count Basie got his name or rather, title, "Count" (Basie is the Count's real family name). John Hammond, the renowned jazz authority and brother-in-law of Benny Goodman, answered the question. "It was a WHB Kansas City radio announcer who said, "There's a Duke of Ellington and an Earl of Garner, we've got to have a Count of Basie.""

Count Basie has that far-away look, yet he always knows where he's at, what's going on and what to do about it. Count Basie is leader of one of the most consistently swinging bands in musical history. He very definitely has always had both feet planted firmly on the ground—except when one of them happens to be tapping slightly in time, which is whenever his ever-swinging band is playing.

For almost half a century Basie's group, without radically changing its style, has remained one of the greatest, one of the most admired bands of all time. The Basie style? Loud, robust and always swinging ensemble sounds, interspersed with fine solos, and the light, infectious piano playing of Basie himself.

Basie and his band originated in Kansas City, a city beloved and respected by true jazz buffs, yet Basie's band has always maintained its popularity largely because it never has played above the heads of its audiences. The band was—like so many—discovered by the same John Hammond who did more than any single individual to promote the brilliant career of Benny Goodman. John could well afford to indulge in his hobby of "discovering" and promoting jazz. He was and is an enormously wealthy man whose hobby is music—jazz, especially—and whose hobby has become in his life time his vocation as well as his avocation. His taste is impeccable and his contribution to American music can never be underestimated either by musicians themselves or by a music loving public.

John Hammond happened to hear the Basie band over the radio one night when he was visiting in Chicago and got the Kansas City station. The result was he made a trip to hear the band in person. The band was playing in the Reno Club and it was great. A little rough in spots, but nevertheless sufficiently great that John Hammond got MCA's Willard Alexander to sign the band up.

It should be explained that many of the black bands in the beginning sounded a little rough, especially in the sax section which was quite often out of tune. The answer lay in the fact that, at that time, many black musicians were unable to afford top-flight instruments and were forced to blow inferior horns. Many of these instruments, no matter how good the player might be and how hard he might try, could not be blown consistently in tune simply because the notes themselves were not in tune.

There was a second reason, also basically economical, for poor intonation. Few black musicians could afford the luxury of prolonged instruction. What is even more important, because of social barriers, very few were able to study with the highly trained and experienced teachers—graduates of top musical schools such as Juilliard in Manhattan or with top studio musicians.

Instead they learned from those who may have been quite competent in what they did teach but who hadn't had the breadth of

119

experience or the concentrated tutelage that had been made available to white instructors and musicians.

The black musician was dependent upon sheer talent, genius, guts and an inborn love of the music which rocked in his soul. He just had to blow it out, like the Angel Gabriel. He blew out his soul and swing was swinging and becoming beautiful music.

When the Basie band was first booked into New York it appeared at Roseland and the Savoy Ballroom but it was in a small club—the Famous Door—that New Yorkers began to hear how great the band really was.

One of the stars who worked with Count Basie was the legendary Billie Holiday—a girl singer whose black beauty was at once compared to that of Lena Horne, by then an established star. Both girls being black and beautiful and both with unique singing styles naturally provoked comparisons. In actuality, there is little resemblance. At times one can discern a little bit of Horne in a Holiday recording, but I, for one, have never heard a projection of Holiday in Lena's singing. Lena, herself, was a great personal admirer of Billie Holiday's singing and whenever she could she went to watch her perform.

But the quality which sustained Lena Horne and which kept her not only unique, but preserved, was her own self-discipline. She never allowed herself to fall into any of the pit-holes which became disaster wells for Billie and her personal weaknesses. In the category of self-discipline and restraint, the only girl singer comparable to Lena is Doris Day. Both were able to by-pass the attentions and the well-meaning but often disastrous overtures of their publics. They avoided indulgence in drink, drugs and kept their sex lives under the close control of their needs. Billie, on the other hand, was unable to control any portion of the emotional area of her own self. The consequences were personal disaster and a great tragic loss to the world of music.

Once again it was the same John Hammond, an ardent supporter of both Billie Holiday and Count Basie, who brought the two stars together. He recalls, "I'd given Count some of Billie's records to listen to, but it wasn't until I almost twisted his arm and took him to Munro's up in Harlem to hear her in person that he decided to hire her."

Billie fitted in perfectly with the band, which included such greats as trumpeter Buck Clayton, Lester Young, tenor saxist Herschel Evans, drummer Jo-Jones and bassist Walter Page and Jimmy "Mr. Five-by-Five," Rushing, Basie's great blues shouter. Unfortunately, Billie never worked many engagements with the Count. The most important engagement was at the Savoy ballroom but the Count always spoke of her reverently. "She was our first girl vocalist and she was beautiful to work with. I used to be just as thrilled to hear her as the audience was." Billie left the Count to go with Artie Shaw who offered her more money. She never had an opportunity to record with the Basie band as she was under contract to Brunswick while Basie was tied to Decca, but she can be heard on two sides taken from a radio broadcast from the Savoy which is included in a Columbia album.

Since the days of the big bands, the Count Basie group flourished with the aid of both Frank Sinatra and Lena Horne, who helped get the group lucrative bookings in Las Vegas and who have appeared with the group in a series of tremendously exciting and successful concerts throughout the land. Despite the radical changes in musical tastes (many of the jazz buffs turned to far more complicated music, while the teenagers, who in the Thirties and Forties had supported the big bands, concentrated almost solely on rock and roll, folk music, and disco). The Basie band continued to blow and boom in the same sort of simple, swinging, straight-ahead groove in which it had slid out of Kansas City in its beginning.

Obviously Lena, Frank and the Count had

been doing something right and had been giving millions of people music they liked to hear.

The thing they were doing was being a part of a true musical world—a world to which they belonged and a world within whose walls they felt real security. All of the musicians whom Lena knew and associated with were men and women who were doing what they liked and liked what they were doing. So today Lena Horne is a composite of the musicians with whom she associated herself.

Certainly one cannot write of Lena Horne and by-pass one of the most delightful and most talented musicians she was ever identified with, Cab Calloway, the man whose very name invokes cries of "Heigh-de-Ho" and "Minnie-the-Moocher."

Or some of the unhip "hip" phrases he used to utter in the Cotton Club days when Lena was a young chorine in the early thirties. Very few people remember or credit him with the great band he organized in the forties. Barry Ulanov, one of music's finest critics, wrote in *Metronone*, 1943, "How many people realize what a great band Cab is leading right now, a band extraordinary in every aspect, in its clean musicianship, its jazz kicks and its brilliant showmanship. Here's one of the magnificent bands of all time!" The band boasted such men of musical genius as trumpeters Dizzy

Gillespie and Jonah Jones and Cozy Cole on drums.

One of the elements which set Cab apart from the other black band leaders was he could afford to and did pay his musicians top salaries which gave them a feeling of financial security and created in them a pride in their work and the type of music they created. Consequently, it was "the tops"—as anyone who ever had the opportunity to hear the band will testify. Cab, like Lena, is a very light skinned "black man" and had very little difficulty in moving in mixed society. He was, in fact, the prototype of the type of black performer European audiences toasted and made to "feel like a king." Cab is a very articulate, appreciative, creative artist. He is extremely alert and possesses a brilliant sense of humor. Of one popular arranger who was known to attract his audience with stentorian introductions, Cab wryly commented, "He comes on like 'Gangbusters' and goes off like 'The Goodwill Hour.' " His own singing ability, beyond his skill of clowning, which he thoroughly enjoys doing, has been very underrated, but his talents have not. Like Lena, when the big bands died, Cab took up a career in the movies and extended himself to the live stage and even the operatic world, creating the role of "Sportin' Life" in George Gershwin's "Porgy and Bess." In this role he toured both the United States and Europe in both the original and revival companies. One of Cab's great qualities is that whatever role he assumes, it becomes him and he in turn, in the public's image, becomes the character.

When he joined Pearl Bailey in the cast of "Hello Dolly" it was difficult from the audience reaction to discern whose show it really was.

Naturally, in the company of such musical greats the knowledge of music was to unfold for Lena Horne, who by her own admission was not in the beginning, a great singer, and who, to this very day, has some reservations about her singing.

It is only realistic to understand that the relationship of Lena Horne and Lennie Hayton had to evolve out of the wonderful world of music which they both inhabited. Had Lena managed to make her first marriage work, it is questionable that there would be any reason for a book to be written about her. She would probably have fallen into the oblivion of many young women of talent and beauty who dropped by the wayside. It took a John Hammond to discover the talent of Lena Horne and it also took a Lennie Hayton to perfect it and place it in the spectrum of the musical world.

Three Lena Horne films, "Cabin in the Sky," "Thousands Cheer," and "Stromy Weather" were all released within a few months of each other and all did well at the box office. If MGM didn't know what to do with her, Fox did, they cast her as the lead in "Stormy Weater" and got themselves a hit.

CHAPTER SIX
MOOD INDIGO
The Composers, the Arrangers, the "Gigs"

In 1923 a few years after Lena Horne was born, an American beauty married to a great American novelist living in Paris said, "I have a hearty liking for jazz music, especially Irving Berlin."

These were the words of the "flapper incarnate" Zelda Fitzgerald, wife of the famous writer F. Scott Fitzgerald, the man who more than any other single person was possibly responsible for creating the mood of the "jazz" era. How much of it was tinsel and how much tallow to "burn at both its ends" while scarcely lasting the night is rather apparent to today's investigative reporter.

Duke Ellington has said, "Jazz is the only word that has no real meaning. We quit using it in 1943." The Duke dislikes being categorized as a jazz musician, because in his very articulate terminology, categorization means segregation.

In actuality, jazz is considered a form of American music. Louis Armstrong recalled that jazz was "ragtime" when he got started. But regardless, it was through jazz and musicians who played what was known as jazz music that an integration of the wonderful world of music occurred. A language used by the musicians—one of the great innovators was none other than Cab Calloway—always loquacious and descriptive in his speech, became a part of the American language.

Finally, one of the early jazz musicians named Mezzy Mezrow brought forth a dictionary which explained to some of the "cats" who didn't "dig" the "jive" just what it was all about.

Ironically, the man who discarded the word made one of the original contributions when as a fifteen-year-old boy he sat down at a piano and played for a group of his schoolmates who were celebrating a birthday party his own original creation titled, "What you Gonna Do

When the Bed Breaks Down?" When Ellington played he was surrounded by "beautiful chicks"—and so he and his band played on and on and on. The boy had no technical musical training though he was from a Baltimore "black" society family. He had shown sufficient artistic talent to win a scholarship to the Pratt Institute. He never followed through on this other natural talent. He stayed with music. It became his life, "his mistress," and he made a unique separation, in his career, among musicians. To the Duke there were two kinds. "Ear cats and school boys." He chose to run with the "ear cats."

Jazz was the world created by such writers as Fitzgerald and Van Vechten based upon a "Jazz Era" that made it possible for such places as the Cotton Club, the Savoy, Roseland, the Palladium, Birdland, etc., and then sundry small intimate clubs to feature black music and black musicians called "jazz" singers and "jazz musicians."

Neither Irving Berlin nor Al Jolson in "black face" qualify as "jazz musicians," but this opinion is not that of the crazy Zelda who frightened Ernest Hemingway into a moment of sobriety by asking if he didn't *really* think that "Al Jolson was greater than Jesus Christ?"

Perhaps "The Jazz Singer" was, and perhaps the music of Irving Berlin is, "great jazz music." Both are *moot* questions, today amusing irrelevant observations.

But we do have a great deal to be thankful for in the wonderful world of music. Jazz did bring to us beautiful music and beautiful people and has possibly helped as much as any single force, including sports, to make an integrated world, especially among the lovers of music, among the artists, who never paid much attention to segregation anyway.

Although Lena Horne came to us from the Cotton Club in Harlem via Noble Sissle's black band and Charlie Barnet's "big" white band, her real musical identity as a "star" commenced with jazz enthusiast John Hammond's appreciation of her latent talents.

Her beauty was one thing, but it takes more than mere physical beauty to create a star. Since Lena came to her "stardom" via Charlie Barnet's big band, she had to contribute something more to the musicians than mere physical beauty. She did. John Hammond spotted it and had Barney Josephson, owner of Cafe Society, give her a "spot" in an intimate, expensive night place that catered almost exclusively to a white, affluent audience which thought, because of its wealth and iconoclasm, that it was an elite audience. To a degree it was. In addition to the wealthy patrons it was frequently by those men and women of the arts who could afford to visit there. Here white composers such as John La Touche, author of "Begger's Holiday" sat alongside black arrangers such as Phil Moore and listened while Lena warbled.

To categorize Lena Horne as a jazz singer is as meaningless as to categorize the "Hope" as a diamond. Anyone who has studied the style of Lena knows that she is a singer so far as her jazz qualification goes. The "Hope" is an enormous diamond and to those few who have been privileged to see it, the stone is in color saphire blue. John Hammond when he "discovered" Lena knew she was "special;" he knew she had "star" quality, but neither he nor any other critic ever segregated her into the category of being a "jazz singer."

Lena confesses that her knowledge of music when she became a vocalist was extremely restricted. Actually she sang what was handed to her without special arrangements or tutelage. Undoubtedly, in the beginning it was her exotic beauty which appealed to audiences. She was fortunate to work with a man of means like Charlie Barnet who was also a dedicated musician and who saw that she got some musical training. It was when composers and arrangers began to see her potential that "special" material was written and submitted to her and in the small cafe downtown in the Village, Lena's looks and beauty eventually got her to a spectacular Broadway production, "Panama Hattie."

But lovers of Lena Horne must always remember that essentially she was singing for "bread"—money to support herself and her little family. Before her Hollywood adventure—or misadventure—and her marriage to Lennie Hayton, Lena was merely a gorgeous instrument of sound. It was as she began to know and understand music and the men who created music that she began to assume the stature of an "artist."

Yet to some music appreciators she blossomed at first sight. Larry Shayne, famous music publisher and the man who brought Dick Haymes to Harry James as the band soloist to replace Frank Sinatra, recalls the first time he heard Lena singing with Charlie Barnet in an engagement at the Apollo Theater in Harlem "Her's was a very special musical talent; she had a style and a projection of material which was completely original. She was beyond specific classification. And, her beauty was so spectacular that it often overshadowed her enormous talent. Many people misjudged her ability and even though they acknowledged that she was—almost from the beginning—a truly great star, they never took the time to analyze her talent; they simply were mesmerized by her exotic beauty.''

When Lena packed up and left Manhattan for Hollywood, where she sang at the Little Troc, the black musical community was not very extensive and those who were there working in films were still carrying on in the tradition of what the white public desired of a black ''jazz'' musician. Bill Robinson was dancing ''buck and wing,'' Ethel Waters was singing ''blues,'' Cab Calloway was reigning as ''The Prince of Heigh-de-Ho,'' Nat ''King'' Cole was in the process of emerging as one of the big male stars of his generation. (He married Maria Ellington, one of Duke Ellington's trio of girl singers. Although she had the same surname she was no kin to the Duke.)

One of the black artists who was a contemporary and friend of Lena's in her Hollywood days was the talented pianist, Hazel Scott. Hazel too, was a ''cafe-au-lait'' beauty and the two girls joined forces at the studios where they worked to promote the further employment of black artists. Hazel played a wicked piano and she was extremely kind to the eyes. She had good musical training and probably would have gone much further in her own career had she not fallen in love with the enigmatic political spellbinder, the Reverend Adam Clayton Powell. When Powell became the first black congressman from New York,

Hazel departed from Hollywood and took her place by the side of her politically ambitious husband. Lena, in the meanwhile, met and fell in love with Lennie Hayton who proceeded to perfect Lena, the star, and to bring her vocal talents to their peak. When Lennie encountered Lena, he must have felt like a man who had been playing a good violin, but who was suddenly given full possession of a Stradivarius.

Lena's musical knowledge was quite virginal when she first encountered Lennie, although she had been associated with nothing but musicians. Lennie was the musical intellectual, Lena the natural genius instrument. Their musical relationship in many aspects can be compared to the relationship of Duke Ellington to his protege and arranger, William "Billy" Strayhorn, commonly and affectionately known as "Little" Strayhorn because of his diminuitive size or "Sweetpea"—a nickname some attribute to Lena.

Billy Strayhorn was one of the truly outstanding musical geniuses in a day when talent was abundant. He came from Pittsburgh and received his musical education at the University of Pittsburgh and the Sorbonne in Paris. He was a pianist and the composer of such well-known pieces as "Take the 'A' Train" which became the band's theme song soon after Strayhorn signed with the Duke. Strayhorn wrote many arrangements for Duke, especially for Ivy Anderson and a handsome baritone named Herb Jeffries.

Little Strayhorn's nickname came from his resemblance to a sweetpea, a tiny dewdrop of a man, his eyes shining brilliantly behind his glasses, his sensitively cut lips which were always saying something wicked or witty. His hands were magic on the piano and before he became the Duke's alter ego, there were many clinkers in the Duke's piano playing. (Actually, the Duke was quite painfully conscious of how badly he played the piano.) After working with Strayhorn, the clinkers disappeared from the Duke's playing.

Little Strayhorn composed a number of extremely musical songs, including two that featured Johnny Hodges, "Day Dream" and "Passion Flower," a lovely opus called "Something to Live For" which Jean Eldridge sang so well with the Ellington band, and "Lush Life" which Billy himself used to sing and which became a hit when Nat King Cole recorded it.

Strayhorn fought a losing battle with cancer and finally succumbed in 1967. It was a great blow to the Duke—almost equal to losing one of his hands.

Much has been written about the Duke's

own casual method of writing, on planes and trains and on the walls of recording studios, yet when something of lasting importance to him was in the making he would spend many hours alone at the piano working in a relatively conventional manner at the business of putting down notes that gave what Sweetpea termed "the Ellington essence." This essence is ubiquitous whether in an original framework for Cootie William's horn or an arrangement of some incongruous pop song. In their day the Duke and/or Strayhorn worked on "Who's Afraid of the Big Bad Wolf?," 'The Waltz You Saved For Me," and an entire album of songs from "Mary Poppins." All came out several sizes larger than life.

In addition to those well-known ditties, "Solitude," "Mood Indigo" and "Sophisticated Lady," there are works by the two men which justify their high-brow identity in addition to music of a lower plateau. Such pieces are "A Drum is a Woman" (written for a TV special in 1957), the controversial "Togo Brava Suite," "Harlem Suite," "New Orleans Suite," "Suite Thursday" (impressions of characters from the writings of John Steinbeck), and "Such Sweet Thunder" (inspired by a dozen Shakespearean sonnets or plays).

The same criticisms that were thrown at Lena Horne by her black peers—the thrust of not being primarily a singer of black music written by black musicians—were hurled at Duke Ellington, although some music critics thought of the Duke as being primarily a master of black music. Certainly in a number of the Duke's works, such as "My People," the sense of racial pride is clear in title and lyrics; but the Duke, like Lena, was too deeply involved with music to take even as much time as Lena did with conscious cause-fighting.

It is not without significance that dozens of nonblack musicians or singers have passed through his ranks, most notably Louis Bellson, drummer and composer and one of the Duke's closest friends along with his black wife, Pearl Bailey.

Both the Duke and Lena are artists who have made their contributions to Afro-American culture and to the 20th Century culture as a whole.

In the days when Lena was singing at Cafe Society Downtown, New York was a veritable pot-pourri of "black and tan" music and musicians who were featured at the intimate little clubs which were to be found not only in the Village but along Fifty-Second Street from Fifth Avenue to Sixth to Cafe Society Uptown in Harlem. Among musicians in the forties, the mood was indeed indigo—and integration. World famous personalities could be found almost nightly in any of the spots which featured American jazz music and singers. Little Strayhorn, surrounded by two strong arm thugs hired by the Duke to protect him and keep him from being robbed or mugged as he wandered from spot to spot and upon occasion was "over-served," would usually end his nightly rounds at Small's Paradise, a famous bar in Harlem. Strayhorn would be propped against the bar, while his libation was being poured by none other than the red-headed, serious-minded black bartender who looked like a jaundiced white thug. The bartender was to become known as "Malcolm X" and under such a name he would go down in history.

On Fifty-Second Street Billy Daniels was to be heard nightly singing "That Ole Black Magic" while black tuxedoed Gladys Bently accompanied him on the piano and sang her own number, "I Ain't Had a Dime Since I Laid It On The Line Fo' Father Divine." Down in the Village at the Bon Soir, Jimmy Daniels—he who had been the "darling," the Van Vechten "Spider Boy" during his residence in Paris where he hosted for Bricktop in her famous bistro—emceed while the audiences delighted in the piano playing of Norene Tate; the shimmy singing of plump as pudding, Mae Barnes; the musical antics of the

Three Flames with the delightful bass-player Tiger Haynes, an import from St. Croix in the Virgin Islands; the calypso voices of Harry Belafonte and Josephine Premice and the folk songs of guitarist, Josh White. Mid-Town at the Blue Angel were performances by Eartha Kitt (in the early fifties) and songbird Thelma Carpenter, while on Fifty-Second Street in Tony's West Side, Mabel Mercer sat proudly under her self-portrait and sang for her own special and dedicated audience, while Bobby Short took over the Bemelman's Room in the swank Hotel Carlyle until, by the seventies, it belonged to him alone.

There was a great deal of talent and a great deal of music and very many good musicians. During this period Lena and Lennie alternated between America and Europe where they became friends with Noel Coward, Vernon Duke, Cole Porter and Igor Stravinsky (who later moved to Hollywood and worked with Lennie and Lena). But, when Lena and Lennie were in Manhattan they could be seen at popular night spots such as The Famous Door where Count Basie held forth.

The Famous Door was one of the best known of the small jazz spots which, until Count Basie appeared there, had only played small jazz combos. It was a small club, approximately twenty-to-twenty-five feet wide and maybe sixty feet deep. Willard Alexander, the MCA scout who had discovered Basie, felt the locale would be an ideal spot for the Count and his music. It had a select and musically sophisticated clientele. The management wasn't persuaded by Willard's enthusiasm for Count Basie and was unwilling to enlarge until Willard suggested they could do much more business if they installed air-conditioning. He offered to lend the club $2,500 for the unit and they booked Basie's band. Basie only got $1,300 a week but radio network officials frequented the club and when they heard Basie, the fame of the Count Basie Band spread like wildfire.

In the mid-forties, one of the most impressive bands to play The Famous Door was Teddy Powell's band. Teddy was a former violinist and guitarist with Abe Lyman and a fairly successful songwriter. A nervous, impatient, but thoroughly likeable man, Teddy wanted to start right at the top. He hired a super press-agent and went into The Famous Door with a green orchestra. He hyped the press agent's publicity and got bookings outside of New York, but the hinterlands were not ready for the Teddy Powell Band. He lost his shirt, succeeded in getting another booking at The Famous Door, but it was cancelled almost as soon as the ink was dry on the contracts.

The owners had gone bankrupt. Teddy Powell managed to scrape together sufficient money to take over The Famous Door and re-opened with his own band. But Teddy Powell's style of music was meant more for dancing than for listening and his stay in his own "gig" was short-lived.

Another Teddy was also a big attraction at The Famous Door for a short while, the band of Teddy Wilson, the man whom no less a person than Benny Goodman called "the greatest musician in dance music today, irrespective of instrument." The band featured vocalist Thelma Carpenter. Its style was very "polite" like Teddy himself. But "polite" colored bands were difficult to sell in those days. "Everybody kept saying we sounded too white." (It seems we've heard that "song" before!) But the listening was good, especially when it featured Teddy's superb piano playing. His theme was "Little Things Than Mean So Much" composed by Wilson, who also did most of the arranging. Perhaps the band remained too polite; perhaps it needed more flash to attract a public that associated excitement with black bands. In 1940 Teddy gave up the band and continued his musical career with small groups playing the kind of music of good taste and distinctive quality which personified both Teddy Wilson, the man and Teddy Wilson, the musician.

It was when Lena Horne was singing at Cafe Society Downtown that she first met Paul Robeson, a man and a musician who was to have an important influence on her inner self and her political personality. He came to hear her and was so impressed by her beauty and her voice that he asked to meet her. Lena, who seldom mingled with the customers, was only too happy to oblige the man who was to a degree a black idol. It is interesting to note that when Count Basie was playing The Famous Door, Robeson also visited him and in 1941 Count Basie recorded a two-sided opus that can hardly be called an epic. Its title, "Big Joe," its vocalist, Paul Robeson.

When Lena first met Paul Robeson he was indubitably the American Renaissance Man of the Twentieth Century. In naming the Rutgers star of his 1918 All-American team, Walter Camp called Robeson "the greatest defensive end who ever trod the gridiron." When Robeson appeared on Broadway in "Emperor Jones" George Jean Nathan described him as "one of the most thoroughly eloquent, impressive and convincing actors" he had ever seen. And after Robeson gave a concert of Negro spirituals in Greenwich Village, Alexander Woolcott acclaimed him the "finest musical instrument wrought in our time."

When he sang the lines "Let me go away from the Mississippi, Let me Go 'way from de white man boss" from "Ol' Man River," you knew that's all Paul Robeson ever wanted. Incontestably he was a moody and complex figure, as passionate and full of rage as "Othello," as vainglorious as "Emperor Jones."

Paul Robeson had a natural sense of rhythm and was born a singing fool. But he had much more, too. He didn't enter Rutgers as America's first black jock mercernary. His father was a runaway slave who became a respected minister; his mother was a Philadelphia schoolteacher. Paul Robeson won a scholarship to Rutgers, fairly and honestly; he also won his class oratorical contest for four years and was elected to Phi Beta Kappa and delivered the commencement speech for the class of 1919.

From there Robeson went to Columbia Law School and received his degree in 1921. That year he also married a bright chemistry student named Eslanda Cardoza Goode, who pointed him toward the theater and managed his career until she died in 1965. He eventually found his way down to Greenwich Village, the Provincetown Players and Eugene O'Neill. His voice and bearing brought powerful roles (Brutus Jones in "Emperor Jones"; Crown in

"Porgy;" Joe in "Showboat" and Othello in Shakespeare's "Othello."

Sportswriters in the perfervid pulp prose of 1918 called him "the colored giant" or "the dark cloud." Rutgers classmates remembered him as a "modest and genial young man." When he soared to national stardom, everyone was glad he wasn't another Jack Johnson, beating up decent white boys and bragging about it or running around with white girls. The world was his oyster—even if the oyster did occasionally have to be served in a separate dining room. (Dr. Vera Dreiser, niece of Theodore Dreiser, author of "An American Tragedy," tells of the dramatic moment when she and her uncle went backstage to visit Paul Robeson when he was starring in "Othello" and was the rave of the theater going world. When they suggested dining at the nearby Russian Tea Room he took them instead to a dining place in the Village where they could dine in peace and together.)

In 1928 Robeson met George Bernard Shaw, who asked him what he thought about socialism. He hadn't thought about it at all, but he began to.

In a 1934 tour of the Soviet Union he was impressed by what he saw as the absence of racial prejudice. His roseate vision would have evoked hollow laughter along the Gulag Archipelago, but what did Paul Robeson know of Stalin's death camps? He did know about Harlem, and about ghettoes and Jim Crow laws and lynchings. And he became determined to bury Jim Crow.

Robeson began to trod the familiar trail of the liberal, from the Welsh coal mines to American union halls to dark Spain, singing "Joe Hill" and "Ballad for Americans" instead of "Ol' Man River." That was fine after the Allied-Soviet pact but something less than acceptable once the Cold War set in. He dug his American grave when in 1949 he told the World Peace Conference, "It is unthinkable that American Negroes will go to war on behalf of those who have been oppressed for generations, against a country which in one generation has raised our people to the full dignity of mankind."

Paul Robeson was one of the first artists to make a stand and issue a public statement on the role of an artist in society. He said, "The artist must take sides. He must elect to fight for the freedom of slavery. I have made my choice."

Racial and economic injustices enraged him, energized him. It was a bad time for blacks in America in the 1930s and '40s when he first met Lena Horne. ("I am never for one moment unaware that I live in a land of Jim

Crow,'' he said at the height of his immensely successful career.) Without question it was Robeson's keen sensitivity to the plight of millions of his people—jobless, landless, hopeless—that led him to his fervent embrace of radicalism. Some of his passion had to penetrate Lena's own consciousness, and some of the bitter tragedy which pursued him must have affected the behavior of Lena and other successful black artists. His plight was unbelievable.

By choice he became a leader a pioneer. Years before activism became an accepted tactic, Robeson spoke and wrote urging blacks to organize en masse, to boycott, to get and use the vote. He was one of the first to link the black struggle in America to the worldwide revolt of black and brown people against their colonial masters. His jeremiads against colonialism and its attendant racism even today carry the sting of a horsewhip.

But Robeson's greatest legacy—especially to people like Lena Horne who knew him and heard him expound privately and in person—was the sense of self-respect and self-worth he helped to recover for his people. At a time when many blacks were conditioned to be ashamed of their color and ignorant of their history, Robeson trumpeted,'' I am proud of my African heritage.'' He studied African languages and folk lore, teaching himself such difficult dialects as Yoruba and Efik. He told his people they were indeed inheritors of a rich non-western culture—oral, intuitive, rhythmical—that had flourished for centuries and had been stripped from them in slavery.

While he was inculcating friends and intelligent black leaders with his knowledge, his own employability in the U.S. plummeted drastically—especially after he took the Fifth Amendment before the McCarthy Committee. Like Lena and Lennie and other famed artists, he retreated to Europe. He spent most of his time in London, but later came home to live in relative seclusion with his sister in Philadelphia. He possessed too subtle and too sensitive a mind not to have noted the irony of his private embattlement versus the embattlements of the flaming sixties. But nothing lured him forth to the new battlefield; his fight was done. The young radicals such as Stokely Carmichael scarcely knew who he was; older whites agreed he was born before his time. His banishment from society was nothing short of a national disgrace. He died in obscurity at the age of 77, surely tired of living and just as surely too bitter to be scared of dying.

Despite the efforts of many prominent artists, including Lena and Lennie, it was not until the 81st anniversary of Paul Robeson's birth that his memory was commemorated by the placing of a star in his honor on the Hollywood Walk of Fame; an honor for which he was nominated by the Screen Actor's Guild and Actor's Equity. Sidney Poitier, who unveiled the Robeson star called himself, "One of the numerous black artists who proudly walk in the shadow of Paul Robeson."

Lena Horne speaks almost reverently of Paul Robeson. "I shall always love that man and be eternally grateful to him for what he taught me." Out of respect, Lena has tried to live up to his ideals.

It has never been an easy task combatting the public pressure in which one has to live up to some sort of an image—a triple threat pressure when one is a celebrity, a Negro and a woman. If, as the years pass, Lena tends to retreat more into herself it is because she prefers to remain where she can "just be myself."

It is in the world of music and among musicians that Lena is most at ease with herself. For someone in love when Lena sings, her songs are all there is to say. It has been so since the beginning and every time she reaches a pinnacle she goes on to top it. "The Jazz Baby" with Phil Moore, the lovely leggy that Lennie Hayton steered on to MGM stardom, the fabled SRO artist of the 1960s in Las Vegas, New York and the capitals of the world, and in the 1970s touring with Vic Damone, Tony Bennett and Count Basie, have all combined to make this lady one of the world's most singularly unusual interpreters of music and lyrics, truly a legend in her own lifetime.

She loves working in concert with Tony and Vic and Count Basie. "I think it's because I like and respect them—we all get along so well. There's none of that show-biz or competitive feeling when we work together. That might be more likely if I worked opposite another woman singer."

Lena's observation is made because of her lack of self assurance about herself as a singer. She has never possessed this quality. She admits that there have been times in her career when she wanted to commit suicide because she could not sound like Aretha Franklin, whom she adores, or Dionne Warwick, whom she admires. She admits: "I read somewhere that Roberta Flack said I might not sound black to some people, but she thought I had a tremendous amount of soul. People never used to say that. I think it's because I have grown and I've made peace with myself and it is very gratifying."

Nevertheless, working for dinner-digesters and drinker-gamblers has never been Lena's style. She makes no bones about being devoted to musicians, who she feels understand her better than others outside their special world. When she was in New York in concert with Tony Bennett, she recorded with Michel Legrand and all the guys—Richard Tee, Cornell Dupree, Ron Carter, Grady Tate—the giants!

One reason for her preference for concert work is the audiences who arrive prepared to sit still and concentrate.

"That's what makes concert work in theaters so great. That, plus the fact that musicians are always so very tender with me, they teach me. When I recorded Michel's songs, which are wonderful but Hell to sing, he taught me how to sing them as they should be sung. And I recorded a song by Ben Fredman, my conductor, who writes a great deal like Lennie."

Even today, when Lena talks about the wonderful world of music, her conversation leads back to Lennie. Lennie arranging songs by Johnny Burke and Jimmy van Heusen, songs by Rogers and Hart, by Cole Porter, songs by a decade of song writers, songs for Lena Horne to sing. "I miss not having Lennie to turn to and say, "Hey, isn't that good!" But Lena is still singing songs for Lena Horne to sing. Her repertoire is endless, just as her style is timeless. In the wonderful world of music it can be said that the unique style which characterizes the singing of Lena Horne will immortalize many songs which otherwise might fade into oblivion. With all of her peers, this is her great contribution. Her devotion to her family, her devotion to her people, her devotion to her self and her art, none equal her devotion to the wonderful world of music. The world in which she found "soul."

Lena with her husband of twenty-five years, musical genius and widely admired Lennie Hayton. The occasion was a New York party in celebration of Lena's first book (done with Richard Schickel), published in 1965.

Lena's disallusionment with Hollywood grew as time passed.
Such instances as having her big production number from the
musical "Zigfield Follies" cut from the film—and the above
publicity shot from the film going unreleased contributed to her
decision to move back to New York.

Cab Calloway with Lena in a publicity still from "Stormy Weather". The idea for the movie came from Lena's hit recording of the song. After the success of the 20th Century Fox film, Lena returned to MGM where she turned down the starring role in the film version of the Broadway hit, "St. Louis Woman" because she felt the script demeaned blacks.

After refusing "St. Louis Woman," Lena was told by MGM that she would not be allowed to play clubs and concerts anymore. And since she much preferred live perfomances to films, it was goodbye Hollywood, at least for a little while.

CHAPTER SEVEN
"If The Shoe Fits, Wear It" -

To most of her friends and intimate associates, Lena Horne is affectionately called "Miss Calhoun."

The year 1971 began a period of personal tragedy for Lena. First her father died of emphysema. Five months later her son, Teddy, died of a rare kidney ailment. Then her husband died. Devasted, she decided to sell the house in Palm Springs. At the time she was quoted as saying she would never own another home. Then she discovered Santa Barbara, California. She'd been there before, of course, as it's only a couple of hours up the coast from Hollywood. The gracious old Spanish colonial city is considered by many to be one of the most beautiful spots in the world. There, among the prominent author, artist and actor residents, Lena felt she could forget her sorrow and just become "Miss Calhoun" in a community which has been the been a quiet retreat for the very famous for many years. Surrounded by the Santa Cruz mountains, the mission-style city overlooks the wide Pacific and the distant off shore Channel Islands. It enjoys not only spectacular scenery but delightful weather most of the year. The plastic people of the Hollywood community are not comfortable in Santa Barbara, an area which wreaks of stability, of permanence. It's, for want of a better word, elegant. It has a quiet, underspoken class.

And Santa Barbara was exactly what "Miss Calhoun" needed when she found her home there.

When daughter Gail separated from Sidney Lumet, Lena moved away from Manahattan and settled in Palm Springs. While she'd said she'd never own another home, once she saw the house in Santa Barbara she bought it, "because I just fell in love with it."

Lena discovered the house driving up the coast from San Diego, where she had just fulfilled an engagement. In her words, the house was "a real story-book house, about one hundred years old." It was once a part of an olive mill.

Miss Calhoun settled into her new home and stored all the memorabilia she had longed to remove from sundry storage bins in sundry warehouses in sundry parts of the world. There was her collection of records, Lennie's old music, her old costumes, tangible reminders of a career which had then lasted more than half a century. There were the graphic souvenirs of a woman named Lena Horne gathered in toto for a woman called Miss Calhoun to study and reminisce about. Into this house the dual personalities merged and become one—the artists who is alternately gregarious and solitary.

Lena Horne is "happy when working with people—especially people I feel close to—dancers, singers, musicians." Miss Calhoun is happy "with my family—or, when I'm alone."

She would enjoy her visting family and her quiet times alone in the beautiful Santa Barbara house for many years. It was not until 1985 that she moved to Washington to be nearer daughter Gail and her grandchildren.

Looking about her home in Santa Barbara soon after she moved there, Miss Calhoun said: "It's very quiet here, very lonely. Yet, I'm quite unafraid. I sit at night, reading or listening to music and I hear the wind whistling through the trees, and it's wonderful."

An old spiritual comes to mind.

    ' 'Steal away…steal away home
    I ain't got long to stay here…
    Green trees are bending,
    Poor sinners trembling
    The trumpet sounds in my soul…
    I ain't got long to stay here…''

A shadow falls across the freckled nose of Miss Calhoun (the tiny bit of pigmentation which contributes to the face of Lena Horn—that one flaw, that one imperfection that true artists require in earthly beauty, the imperfection which becomes a source of beauty and recognition unto itself), and she furrows her classic brow as she relaxes and welcomes the ghosts awaiting their cues in the life of Lena Calhoun Horne.

"But, Mama, I want to be an actress!"

"Just you listen to me, Edna dear, there's no future for you in acting!"

The two apparitions are a young, slim, gentle girl of fifteen years, delicately pretty as she stands with tears in her eyes pleading her cause to the older spirit, a prim, proud-visaged woman whose strong features are the outward symbol of an aristocratic ancestry. The characters are Miss Calhoun's young mother, Edna, and her Grandmother Scottron.

Grandmother Scottron was a schoolteacher whose husband was the first Negro member of the Brooklyn Board of Education. Theirs was a home of refinement and culture. They both knew the futility of their young daughter's ambitions. They knew the theater was no place for any black person. "Even black roles are played by white actors in blackface make-up!" So long as Grandfather Scottron was alive, Edna would never set foot upon the stage. She would have to be content sitting at home, reading aloud her favorite role, "Cleopatra," and wait for some young ambitious black man to ask for her hand in marriage.

But Grandfather Scottron did not live out his full life expectancy and when he died, Grandmother Scottron found it impossible to continue the payments on the house. She succumbed to Edna's pleas and allowed her daughter to "try-out" for The Lafayette Players where she was hired as a dancer in the chorus.

Edna was much too pretty to go unnoticed, especially by the young gentlemen who frequented the "backstage" in the role of stage-door Johnnies. One, a handsome black bachelor already spoiled by too many women, fell madly in love with her. After his first interview with Grandmother Scottron convinced Teddy Horne that the only way he would win Edna was to take her hand in marriage. The fact that both Teddy and Edna were too young to face the responsibility of marriage seems to have been overlooked not only by Edna's mother but by Teddy's parents, the Hornes, who were equally respectable and unusually well educated for blacks of the period.

Teddy's father was a combustion inspector for the Brooklyn Fire Department and before coming north he had been a high-school principal in Nashville, Tennessee. His wife was a woman of a wide background and education. They were progressive and active in community projects. Their home on Chauncey Street was a home which reflected the upper-middle class standards of the century. Verdi's music was played on the gramaphone, books of history and literature filled the bookshelves.

Teddy's mother was one of the founders of the newly organized National Association for the Advancement of Colored People.

They were fully cognizant of what had been the fates of their ancestors and were dedicated to improving the lot of their descendants. They knew some of the history of slavery, but they lived in the hope that the hatreds and resentments were deeply buried in the past. They looked to the future of the American Negro. It is conceivable that their intellectual interests and pursuits made true communication between young playboy Teddy and his lovely wife, Edna, null and void.

The young couple lived with Teddy's parents on Chauncy Street in Brooklyn where baby Lena Calhoun Horne was born on June 30, 1917. World War I had been fought and attitudes between black and white people were due for considerable changes. Lena's father, Teddy, became acutely aware that he was his father's son, a Negro in America. That was the challenge. He grew restless in the upper-middle class environment of his parents. He was not prepared to accept the conventionality of a monogamous marriage. He cast his eyes West and left to go to make a life for himself in Pittsburgh. Edna and three-year-old Lena moved to Harlem, where Edna resumed her career with the Lafayette Players.

Baby Lena adored her mother who carried her with her to all of her performances. Baby Lena was an unofficial member of the first black theatrical company, where the actors performed purely for the love of acting. The pay was very bad and the shows were staged anyplace where Negroes were allowed to enter the theater. The places were few and far between.

"Edna, get that kid out of here!"

On the whistle of the wind come the words, "I ain't got long to stay here . . ."

Miss Calhoun shivers slightly. The voice is

that of one of the other actors, ordering Edna to keep her bothersome "kid," who delighted in "miming" the players, remembering their lines upon occasion when they were unable to remember them; being a "precocious little brat" who like her lovely mother, Edna, "talked so good!" Mama saw to that. Little Lena talked with perfect diction.

The theaters where blacks could enter were mostly in some of the larger cities in the South, in the Negro ghettoes. Theaters like the Beale Street Palace in Memphis, Tennessee, were exceptional in that they were real theaters—even if they catered to black audiences and had only black performers. In this particular theater, white patrons were allowed admission on Friday nights—only to sit in the "box-seats." The whites rarely came to see performances of any blacks except musicians and singers such as Bessie Smith. They missed seeing performers like Rose McLendon, (whose acting ability and beauty was extolled by Alexander Wolcott as "the lost loveliness that was Duse!"), because segregation was absolute in the American theater south of the Mason-Dixon line. Performers such as Edna Horne, working in all black stock companies, performed more often for such managements as Silas Greene's Tent Show than in legitimate, black theaters. And, if conditions in the theaters were sleazy and filthy, the places in which the performers were housed were abominable in most instances.

It was on tour with her beloved Mama that Lena received the scars which were to remain with her throughout her life, scars which she later attempted to conceal with the professional make-up of cool cophistication.

It was during these very formative years that little Miss Calhoun, who had been born into black bourgeoise society, became acquainted with "the other side of the railroad tracks." She learned the taunts of "whitey" hollering, "If you're smart, Nigger, you'll stay in your place!" Even when Edna tried to locate a home for herself and Lena when she had steady employment in Miami—in the "better Negro section"—they were refused housing because Edna was "an actress!" In the "Bible Belt," among the illiterate and highly religious blacks, the word was synonymous with "whore" or "prostitute" as it was among the same class of ignorant whites.

The other side of the tracks meant housing in a shack with a sagging porch, broken stairs, no plumbing, only an "outhouse" where the "sugar wagon" rolled by to clean up the excrement. Lena learned that "white folks is the meanest people in the whole world" and she was advised by the owner of one of the boarding houses in which she and Edna stayed, "L'il girl, don' evah let no white man know what you all is thinkin'."

It was during these touring years that Lena became acquainted with some of her own relatives. Some were kind and offered tender loving care . . .

The voice of Uncle Frank rolls like the deep waves of the Pacific swashbuckling fearlessly against the coastal rocks of Miss Calhoun's Santa Barbara "story-book house."

"Remember, baby, be a good student first."

Uncle Frank was a school teacher in Atlanta, a proud man, a good man.

But there were others.

Voices of kids, taunting, angry voices teasing:

"Yaller, yaller . . . you got a white Daddy . . . yaller . . . ."

"Shamey! Shamey! You got a white Daddy . . . Your Mama's a whore!"

Miss Edna's voice of perfect diction admonishing; "Shame! Shame on you for teasing a little girl! Lena's just as colored as you!"

Wiping away the salty tears, Edna, soothing with words, "You're black, honey. Your Daddy's black. You've got everything to be proud of. You've got something special."

So Lena learned that she was "colored."

She was beginning to learn there were a good many shades to the spectrum. But she did not have the slightest idea of what being colored would mean to her, to Lena Calhoun Horne.

There is cruelty in every society. Miss Calhoun discovered this when she lived with Grandma Horne and was enrolled in the Ethical Culture School in Manhattan. Lena's grandmother, Cora Calhoun Horne, was and still is a formidable ghost-form hovering over granddaughter Lena. She was the first person to place order and discipline in the daily existence of the girl. She was the first person to instill a sense of pride in her self and her projected image. But Lena's world was almost shattered when some of her schoolmates chided her with the words, "If it wasn't for your Grandmother Horne you wouldn't be *nobody!*"

Looking at the pictures of the pretty young Lena with her round, dimpled, smiling face, it is difficult to believe that underneath was developing a shy, frightened girl, a girl whose adolescent personality was amost destroyed by constant moving from place to place, by subjection to an almost unbelievable number of different people. All of the ups and downs endured by Edna and young Lena were suffered during Lena's most impressionable years. It is when Miss Calhoun revisits these years and looks at the characters she encountered that we see the emergence of the Lena Horne we know today.

"The trumpet sounds in my soul . . .
I ain't got long to stay here . . . ."

The quality of being termed "a lady" by all with whom Lena Horne throughout her long career coped, assumes the physical pose in Miss Calhoun, as if she is rehearing from the far distant past the words of her favorite aunt with whom she lived for a part of her youth. "Just remember, chile, if you're truly a lady, you can be a lady anywhere." This thought buried itself in the depths of her personality and contributed to many of Lena Horne's actions and comments about life. Like the time she got a telegram asking her to protest because of the Josephine Baker incident at the Stork Club, and she didn't do anything. Lena didn't do anything, not because she wasn't upset about the incident, but because she herself wouldn't have been caught dead in the Stork Club and she just assumed that Josephine Baker knew what a cheap joint it was, too.

Cheap joints were not, nor have they ever been, Miss Calhoun's favorite hang-outs. By the time she had passed her years of puberty, she had her goals set on traveling through life as a lady in a lady's manner.

In 1931 Edna Horne remarried. This time her husband was a Cuban named Michael Rodriguez. Edna remarried at a period when conditions were beginning to change for black performers. Plays such as "In Abraham's Bosom" and "Green Pastures" were being enacted by black performers in white theaters for white audiences. Even "de Lawd" (originally a white plantation owner) in Marc Connelly's adaptation of Roark Bradford's collection of short stories, "Old Man Adam and His Chillun" a humorous narrating of the Creation by a country preacher-man, was enacted to rave reviews by Rex Ingram, a light-skinned black actor.

Minstrel shows had come to an end and such groups as The Lafayette Players were doomed. White producers had discovered gold in the black talent which was waiting to be exploited.

Edna Horne Rodriguez was never pleased with her failure to succeed in her chosen career as an actress and she joined the roster of many famous stage mothers, although Lena customarily remained silent about the role her mother played in her career.

Little Lena who had been the exacting and exciting child "mime," had become shy and filled with stage fright. She had retreated more into the world of reading rather than pretending and acting. Except for a visit backstage in 1931 at the Capitol Theater in Brooklyn to obtain an autograph from Cab Calloway, who was an idol not only of young Lena, but of every teenager of that time, there is little, if anything theatrical among Miss Calhoun's adolescent souvenirs. It is almost indicative, however, that even at so early a date the beauty and charisma of the young Lena Calhoun Horne was sufficiently impressive to make a lasting impression upon the man who was later in life to become a dear friend and mentor.

It was Edna, who having found no real financial security in her new marriage, prevailed upon Lena to help contribute to the family support by trying out for a chorus job at the Cotton Club. Here the prerequisites were primarily youth and, for the chorus, "tall, tan and terrific." The nearer to the color white the better the job. Young Lena Calhoun Horne had all of the endowments for becoming a chorine and did. There in the youthful scrapbook is Lena kicking her heels, waving her feathers, and smiling that infectious smile as the camera catches a flash photo of the dancing Nicholas Brothers.

While Lena rehearsed, Edna sat on the sidelines in the wings. Eliza Webb, the dance directress, issued instructions. "Dig you on a deuce

168

of brights, gimme about twelve chimes . . ."
Edna seldom budged, but kept time with her
feet. It was her world and whenever the opportunity presented itself she pushed the name of
her daughter into the hands of any producer,
but she was thwarted at almost every turn. Her
companions of former days when she was on
the stage warned her, "Who would want to see
a Negro ingenue?"

She looked at the shining face of Lena. In
her heart she knew someone would. She turned
deaf ears to those advisors who suggested with
full significance the meaning of their words,
"The thing you want to do, Edna, is get this
child to Europe!" In short, find a rich white
"daddy." Reversal of script. Make the white
man pay and pay and pay for the exotic off-
spring of the white rapist and the black slave.
For services rendered, gold and diamonds.
Why not?

Actually, the fault lay not in Edna's ambitions and plans—she was Lena's official
coach, chaperone and agent—but in Lena's
own lethargy.

Miss Calhoun stares out of the window of
the "story-book house" and recalls while
watching "the green trees bending . . . ."

"My problem was I never really wanted to
go on the stage—not after I was a tiny mite.

I'm real family folk and I always fantasized that someday my mother and me and my kids would all live in this great big old family type home somewhere in New York or in Georgia and just be a family. But my mother didn't have that kind of a life and I don't know why in the Hell I expected it!"

By the time Lena Horne had reached the Cotton Club, Miss Calhoun had made up her mind that she was going to live without being loved. She had learned to live alone in an isolated way and most importantly she had come to her own peace with the conclusion that no one would ever really love her regardless of her color. The mold for the gorgeous iceberg had been set. Racial and personal prejudice were synonmous.

Finally Edna did manage to get her daughter a song to sing and when Lena came off stage, her peers—although most of the girls were older than she—greeted her with the arch question, "Who does your Mother know around here, Lena? You sure didn't get to sing that song with your voice!"

"Steal away . . . steal away home
 I ain't got long to stay here . . . ."

Even with her peers on the stage of the Cotton Club where Broadway producers, New

York debutantes, hoods and rich white johns came nightly, there was no sense of permanency for Lena. Not even the comforting words of the show's producer, "That Horne kid's got a lot of talent," were reassuring, even though they were being said to one of the very successful black musicians of the day, Noble Sissle.

The words could hardly have been reassuring after Mike, Lena's step-father, asked for a change in her contract since she was now singing a solo in addition to dancing. He was ushered into the men's toilet where a couple of the thugs who worked for the club's owners held his head in the toilet bowl until he agreed to re-sign the contract on the terms negotiated earlier.

Fear set into the bodies of Edna, Mike and young Lena and paralyzed them. The parents realized that Lena had been signed to what virtually amounted to a lifetime contract. While Lena was dancing, Noble Sissle came and spoke to Edna, who weepingly told him what had taken place. The trio was helpless and entrapped. Even Edna, who had continued urging Lena to do her very best because she was "getting the best training in the world" was defeated. Noble Sissle followed young Lena, being escorted by one of the two thugs to her dressing room, where he put a protective strong arm around the frightened girl, "Don't pay him no mind, Baby. Just go on and finish your show like always. When it's time to leave and go home, just walk off the stage and don't come back. Hear?"

Lena heard. When her act was finished, she walked into the custody of Edna and Mike who literally kidnapped the fancily costumed girl away from the Cotton Club.

Lena as Gilda, the Good Witch of the North, in the film of "The Wiz" a musical based on L. Frank Baum's classic "The Wonderful Wizard of Oz." For many of us Lena's performance was the extreme highlight of the film, which also starred Diana Ross, Michael Jackson and Richard Pryor.

CHAPTER EIGHT

*"The Artist's True Position
Is That Of An Observer."*

Duke Ellington

Miss Calhoun, sitting pretty in her Santa Barbara home, surveying the life and times of Lena Calhoun Horne, becomes the artist consumate. Not only because of her own talent but because of her involvement in the music of America from the 1920s (when she toured with her mother) until the present. Few artists can match such a record.

Harry James, Frank Sinatra, Buddy Rich, Ella Fitzgerald and Count Basie were some of the entertainers who spanned, more or less, as long a period. Most survived the transitions of musical trends without a major break in their careers. Louis "Satchmo" Armstrong and Edward Kennedy "Duke" Ellington probably enjoyed the longest careers; both stepping into the jazz scene more than a half century before their deaths. Both played the music of Scott Joplin and saw the transition from ragtime, to blues, to sophisticated jazz.

A few of the old-timers, like pianist Eubie Blake and blues singer Alberta Hunter, enjoyed revived popularity in old age. Their ages as well as their musical talents attributed to their new-found stardom. Eubie Blake had a Broadway musical named in his honor and Alberta Hunter scored a movie in 1979. The accomplishments of all these people is indicative of the creative force and longevity of the musician and his music.

Regardless of the performer, the melody lingers on. Some melodies belong as much to the artist who introduces the words and song to the public as to the composer.

Few artists have been able to survive the changing political and social changes represented in the past fifty years. Lena Calhoun Horne is one of the exceptions.

To look with absolute objectivity at Lena Calhoun Horne and see the radiantly beautiful woman is to stare in amazement. She has worn the years with such finesse that today—especially upon the stage—she seems even more glamorous and exotic than she did in her youth.

It was none other than Quincy Jones, one of the century's outstanding musical talents who best expressed a belief to explode the typically American—or rather Hollywood—youth complex.

Quincy said, "Talent and ablility are neither young nor old. Agedness is only related to chronology. Without knowhow, nobody is anything."

When you mention Lena Horne's age and eternal beauty, Miss Calhoun laughs as she confesses, "Honey, I've been seeing a deterioration set in since I was thirty. I got myself set up for being old. How would I describe myself? Five foot five with a big behind and a big mouth."

In actuality Lena's large hips have always been the only physical problem with which she has had to cope, and overcoming that "problem" has been a relatively simple one with the world of coutouriers at her disposal since she first stepped from the chorus line at the Cotton Club to sing with Nobel Sissle's famed Society Band.

Sissle had an innate desire to make white people just as conscious of black beauty as of black music. As a dance band for white people his was one of the most popular. He was the favorite bandleader of the famed dancing Castles, Vernon and Irene, the couple who made ballroom dancing the rage during the Twenties. Sissle was a highly intelligent man who was extremely conscious about appearances and he was fully aware that the look of the Castles attributed as much to their success as their Terpsichorean skills. When he took young Lena under his wing, he hired the best designers to dress her and to enhance her youthful beauty.

Sissle dressed Lena in the fashion set by woman of wealth and social standing. There was to be nothing "show girl" about her looks ever. In any case, Lena's inate good taste would have prevailed even without Sissle.

Lena's audition song was the sophisticated "Dinner for One, Please, James." It was perfect for Sissle's band—and his audience—and he hired her on the spot. He renamed her Helena Horne and they hit the road.

Later, in an interview, Miss Calhoun recalled: "I couldn't sing jazz and I couldn't sing the blues and I couldn't understand why Sissle wanted me at first. But he set out to mold me to be an asset to his band, and an attraction to his audience. It was a good job but the touring—remember I was very young—

176

was rough. We played the top clubs and theaters but we often had a hellva time finding a place to stay. It was Jim Crow times and while we were welcome in the best white clubs, we were not allowed in the white hotels, not even in the back door.''

Lena was easily acceptable by fans of the band. None of her features were considered Negroid, yet the very features that have sustained her beauty through the years are ethnically inherited. There were no face lifts, silicone transplants, body sculpture evidences. She did not change her looks as have some of the black stars of today.

One woman, wife of a famous composer, maintains that Lennie insisted that Lena have a ''face job'' done when they resided in Europe in the 1960s. It was supposedly ''not a lift,'' but a highly polished sculpting of her natural good features, a high-lighting. The second oral gossip tid-bit implied that Lena's age is ten years more than admitted, and that Lennie, was determined to keep Lena ageless and had her subjected to the treatments of the famous Dr. Franz Niehaus at his famous clinic in Bevey on Lake Nana in Switzerland, where he reputedly contributed to the longevity and youthful appearances and behavior of such notables as Bernard Baruch, W. Somerset Maugham, Charles Chaplin, Gloria Swanson, etc. The glandular injections, if they were administered to Lena, were indeed miraculous in view of the fact that they also altered her date of birth, Cotton Club "jail-bait" employment contract, and many other legal documents that attest to the veracity of her given birth date. This author repudiates all such talk as erroneous, and beneath editorial consideration.

Miss Calhoun observing Lena's beauty—as if it were a segment of another being—says, "I come from good stock. I inherited good bones. My mother was a great beauty."

A picture of Edna Horne testifies to the truth of this statement and to the reason why Miss Calhoun has never considered Lena Calhoun Horne an exceptional beauty. It is a psychological factor which enters into the evaluation—especially female—of the physical beauty of the off-spring of a famous beauty. Not even today, with most of the world having proclaimed the beauty of Lena Horne will Miss Calhoun acknowledge that her mother's beauty was not superior.

"And," Miss Calhoun continues, "my father, was—to me—one of the most beautiful men I have ever seen."

Again, a photograph of the young Teddy Horne, who was regarded as being "too handsome for his own good," substantiates Miss Calhoun's observation.

Proudly Miss Calhoun adds, "One of my father's grandmothers was a full-blooded Blackfoot Indian!"

In truth, Lena Calhoun Horne never believed in the "sexy image" anyway. Perhaps, unconsciously, she felt it degrading.

"Audiences used to think every black dame was a hot, sexy number, and all I was ever really interested in was seeing to it that my bills were paid and my kids got a good education."

The career of Lena Horne was never an ego-pleasing thing. She was always working because she had someone to support, Miss Calhoun reminds us:

"I didn't used to feel my audiences at all...not at all. I was always just going on and doing my job. I was the breadwinner and that's how I happened to win the bread."

In truth, Lena Horne never changed. She doesn't want to feel that she belongs to the audiences any more than they belong to her, but she has come to realize how many stresses they share in common, how many needs the one fulfills for the other.

For the moment Miss Calhoun is observing the pictures of her father, Teddy, through whom she met her first husband, Louis Jones.

That was in Cleveland, Ohio, during the Christmas season of 1936, where the Sissle band was playing, and Joe Louis was fighting Johnny Risko. Lena was nineteen and Louis Jones, who had come from Pittsburg as her father's traveling companion, was twenty-seven, active in politics and ready to get married and settle down. One look at Lena and he felt he'd come to the end of his search for a suitable wife.

With a few weeks off after the Christmas holidays, Lena returned to Pittsburg to visit her father—and Louis Jones, who was also a minister's son, just happened to live there.

There was an upper class black society in Pittsburg. This group formulated their lifestyles after the blacks who resided in Washington, D.C. They were similar to the Calhouns, the Scrottons and the Hornes of Brooklyn, the families which had created Lena Calhoun Horne. The missing ingredient was the element of the theater which Edna had injected into the family, the element which had really tutored Lena for a career but not as a young first wife.

The culture of this group of blacks was middle-class, and though they were segregated into black ghettoes, they were no more conscious of their segregation than were the European Jews who resided in Jewish ghettoes. But they were daily becoming fully cognizant of the economic strife which was brewing among the sundry ethnic groups settled in the city.

The blacks and the Poles were vying for jobs, and the more intelligent and better educated blacks were becoming aware that they were fighting a losing battle. The Poles were going to outnumber them and win. They became acutely aware of the mounting tensions and when they saw their pursuit for knowledge being restricted to black colleges, to black public schools where the facilities were inferior, they began to wonder if the answer lay in book learning.

It was in the Belmont, Teddy Horne's hotel that different elements of Pittsburg black men met and discussed their fates. It was also there that Louis Jones paid court to Lena Horne the first few weeks of 1937. By the time she was ready to go on the road again with the band, they'd decided to marry.

There were a few snags. "It's the end of your life," Edna told her daughter. Sissle pretty much agreed that Lena's career, once she was married, would be finished. Even her father was opposed to the marriage. Jones was a friend but not the man, in his opinion, to become his daughter's husband.

Regardless, they were married at the home of one of Louis' brothers a few weeks later.

Pittsburgh was a new experience in black living for Miss Calhoun, who had given up her promising career to be the wife of the proud young politician, Louis Jones—"the best catch in Pittsburgh." The marriage, which was short-lived, opened Miss Calhoun's eyes to the existence of another human being within her self-identity, the urban Northern Negro.

Undoubtedly there were advantages to the life of the urban northern black as compared to that of the southern rural black, but the prices paid for the slim advantages were even more demoralizing than the ostentatious form of segregation which existed in the South and which in time would help surface the black man's plight.

The years spent in Pittsburgh with the political and athletic cronies (all black) of her husband and father, who had become quite bitter over the plight of blacks in general, made Miss Calhoun fully conscious of her identity— that of an urban northern black, who as a group were more cynical than southern blacks.

The cynicism which became identified with Lena Horne was but a part of the northern cynicism which was a result of half-promises that were frequently and quite blatantly broken.

Southern blacks didn't get promises from the whites so the idealism and the aspirations remained untainted with the kind of suspicion blacks who lived in such cities as Pittsburgh came to feel.

It was as a result of these broken pledges that the northern black became involved in political and legal battle, which they, as individuals, could not wage but organizations such as the N.A.A.C.P. and CORE could. In analyzing Lena Horne's failure as a young wife to her Pittsburgh husband and father of her two children, Miss Calhoun senses the suppressed guilt which finally, years later, forced the artist to take her stand and become an activist in the black revolution.

When Lena left Pittsburgh and Louis Jones, she found refuge singing with Charlie Barnet and his band—a perfect group for the further development of Lena Horne, the beauty and the artist. It was during this period that Miss Calhoun formulated her advice for eternal youth and beauty.

"My advice is find some time to be alone—or with people you feel close to. Then you can be beautiful and stay beautiful."

It worked and continues to work for Lena Horne.

She spent most of her non-working hours, as well as her working hours, with people she trusted—musicians. She developed her musical taste and yet, Lena Horne never actually studied music per se. She never did learn to read music, nor does she play a musical instrument. Yet, she incorporates in her being the best of music through the last five decades.

Lena has often been audibly critical of many musicians, especially the "overly educated." Her criticism is usually accurate and the same as that reached by men like Leonard Feather, John Hammond and other critics.

She expresses her distaste in simple language. "You know the trouble with that cat is he knows too much music. He reads it but he can't feel it. He's too busy with sharps and those tired old flats."

Her observations are similar to those of the young Duke Ellington (and, also, Billie Holiday) who chose the music of the "ear cats."

Lena's criticism is not only justified in the field of music, but it pertains to almost all of the arts—the over-educated painter, for example. Not until an artist breaks with the conventional pedantic mold does his work become interesting, as in the case of such noted artists as Jackson Pollack and Pablo Picasso. It is perhaps Lena's "good ear" attuned to Lennie's academic skills that made the good combination of arranger and singer, just as the combination of the Duke and the academically trained Billy Strayhorn produced the Duke's masterpieces.

In music, there is definitely a need for the hearing ear, especially in the case of a singer. All of the voice training in the world cannot produce a finished singer if that singer is not basically an "ear cat." The Duke once told Lena that his music was involved in his hours of travel "on the road." Once, driving in the early hours of dawn, the Duke had his driver stop while he sat and listened to a symphony of wild birds singing in the wooded forests adjoining the highway. It was his ear that could translate this natural beauty of sound to a man-made intrument and incorporate it into his work.

It is Lena's "good ear for listening" that made her popular with her fellow musicians, many of whom, from the classical world as well as from the world of jazz, have trusted her judgement of their works.

For Example, of no less a musical genius than Richard Wagner, Lena shakes her head tilting toward the listening ear and comments, "He sounds awfully tubby. His music is big and fat sounding!"

Lovers of Mozart, applaud!

She learned that art is a skill and her skill was perfecting almost through a form of musical osmosis a style which became unique-ly the style of Lena Horne—and the style is characterized by the woman, Miss Calhoun.

Perhaps, it is the early "mime" quality of the child, Lena, that has kept Miss Calhoun from being either jealous or overtly critical of other women singers. She is fully aware of her impact upon them—in her dress, in her presentation, in her actual manner of singing.

Yet, she has assiduously avoided socializing with her peers, "I just don't have time..."

Miss Calhoun shivers and says, "Lena Horne is like the Duke, like Billy Strayhorn said of him. 'He doesn't live in the past, he rejects it, at least as far as his own past accomplishments are concerned.'"

But Lena knows the past will always be remembered. Part of her beauty lies in the fact that she has come to terms with the past, lives in the present and has her eye on on the future.

What will it hold for Lena Horne?

Lena Horne has special songs which are identified with her—songs that made her a legend; "Stormy Weather," "Surrey With The Fringe On Top," "Hello, Young Lovers," the Beatles "Blackbird," and Jimmy Webb's, "Didn't We?"

"Honey, I can't stand to watch myself on television. I get critical. I get nervous. The only way for me to do it is to have two martinis before I turn on the set."

"I saw 'Cabin In The Sky' on television one night and couldn't stay with it for the end. There I was, acting the ingenue, a fluttery, pretty thing. It brought back a lot of memories, mostly that being an ingenue, a fluttery, pretty thing wasn't at all what I felt inside. I could have died when I saw it."

But she didn't. She turned the dial to another channel until she found an old Charles Laughton film. Miss Calhoun hugs her knees to her body.

"I love old movies. I love Charles Laughton!

"But I want to sing the new numbers, the new stuff. Every time I do, I get a lot of flack. Audiences aren't ready to see me that way. They forget I'm listening to what's going on today, too."

Miss Calhoun pauses and continues; "The Duke once told me his reward was in hearing what he had done. I guess that's mine, too, but I've never been what is considered a popular recording artist. I listen to my recordings and get some sort of an idea what I am. Something that was created for both sound and sight. Out of sight, I ain't no genius, but the Duke? Listen!"

Reminded that Duke Ellington once named her as his favorite singer, Miss Calhoun roars with gusty laughter. "His favorite singer? You gotta be kidding. Me? The Duke always said 'The one I'm enjoying at the moment, that's my favorite canary!'"

And he was right.

Is Miss Calhoun aware that there is a growing Lena Horne cult?

187

"I did hear you right, didn't I? Cult? Why? Where from? What makes a Lena Horne song?"

Miss Calhoun pauses and grins, displaying her beautiful teeth. "Like the Duke said, 'It ain't the notes, Baby, it's who they're written for.'"

And by whom they are arranged. Thereby hangs a tale, and it "ain't no old wives tale," chuckles Miss Calhoun.

Early in 1981 Lena opened at New York's Nederland Theater in "Lena Horne, The Lady and Her Music." Shown greeting her on opening night are Elizabeth Taylor and Cab Calloway. The show played New York two years, then went on an international tour that lasted nearly three years!

Once she resumed working after Lennie's death, Lena toured with Count Basie, Vic Damone, Alan King and others in theaters and clubs around the world. Here she poses with Alan King for a Las Vegas Caesar's Palace publicity photograph.

Sarah Vaughn presenting Ella Fitzgerald with the Grammy Award. Sarah, born six years after Ella (1918) got her start as a singer the same way Ella had, by winning one of the famous "Harlem Amateur Night" contests. Lena Horne enjoyed a "mutual admiration society" friendship with both.

Lena Calhoun Horne with daughter Gail Lumet Buckley, mother of Lena's two granddaughterrs, Jennie and Amy Lumet. Gail's family biography, "The Hornes, An American Family" was honered as "a special chronicle of the American scene."

"Lena Horne: The Lady and her Music" was filmed and presented by PBS. 'Tis said that this publicity still from the progra
is one of Miss Calhoun's favorite photos of Lena Horne.

CHAPTER NINE
The Drum Is A Woman

Miss Calhoun fingers a photograph of a smiling Lena Horne returning to America with her husband, Lennie Hayton. Of all the photographs in the collection, this is the one which expresses the emotions of love, security, happiness. Lena is smiling at the world with Daddy's arms protecting her.

Daddy, Lennie Hayton, was indeed a beautiful man in every aspect of the word. Even two decades since his heath it is almost impossible to find someone who will utter an unkind word about the man.

If music was the Duke's mistress and Lena's lover, then it was Lennie Hayton's raison d'etre. In the world of music he was almost too knowledgeable. He played, he composed, he arranged, he conducted. In Lena, he found the perfect medium of expression. The sound of music was his sound of love and when the two met, he converted the "living icicle" into a "velvet touch of love."

"I never knew what love meant until I met Lennie. I didn't dare to love."

Miss Calhoun recounts two grandmothers who were issues of white men and black slave girls. Miss Calhoun was reared to believe, "A white man will sleep with you, but he won't marry you. You can bear his children, illegitimately, but you and his off-spring become modern day Hagars adrift in the wilderness. No laws exist to protect you."

Lena and Lennie were something special. She acknowledges the rumors that all was not always quiet on the western front of their Palm Springs residence.

Lena gave Lennie a hard time. "I didn't dig a lot of the cats he liked. I didn't want them around me. As much as I loved Lennie, I just didn't care for a lot of his friends. I used to ask myself. . .is it because they're white or is it because I don't like these cats? I still don't know the real answer."

Miss Calhoun, today, looks objectively at the long marriage of Lena Horne and Lennie Hayton—a marriage, which for the most part was highly successful, at a time when such a union was inconoclastic and could have been threatening to both careers. (In fact, even Lena admits that the marriage was more harmful to Lennie's career than to hers. In reality, it advanced hers because "Daddy" gave her the protection, the isolation, the love she had always needed and had never before experienced.)

"I reckon I could have stayed at home and just been a good wife to Lennie and a good mother to my children. But, I couldn't stand by and see Lennie support children who were not his. (Actually, Lena's son had been so brainwashed against Lennie by his father, Teddy Horne, that true compatibility between the two never did occur.) Financially, Lennie was certainly capable of supporting all of us in whatever manner we chose—but it was not in my bones to be comfortable in such a role."

Miss Calhoun muses, "Folks, dummies, you get the picture, used to ask me how I felt when I looked at TV and saw white policemen knocking down Negro women with fire hoses and then turned and looked at my husband watching the same picture and see that he is white. How dumb can you be? This kind of question is just as stupid and unfortunately just as normal as the people who make it. Don't they understand that when you look at people you love—husband or friend—you don't see color? It so happens that Lennie Hayton was the kindest person I ever knew. And I—if no one else was—was aware that his reaction to savagery was just as strong, if not stronger than mine."

Lennie Hayton was the most important person in Lena's life.

The importance of men in the life of Lena Horne cannot be underestimated, nor misunderstood in view of the strong influences of both her grandmothers and her own mother, Edna. Lena Calhoun Horne is essentially a man's woman created by men for their special enjoyment. The beautiful doll with a song in her heart was originally a creation of Noble Sissle, featured by Charlie Barnet and developed into the finished product by Lennie Hayton. Few female singers have had such an impressive coterie of male artists interested in their careers; especially male artists without ulterior motives, for although Lena's name has been liked professionally with many men, it has been remarkable devoid of romantic association with men.

Once during World War II, when she and Joe Louis were the idols of the black G.I.s, (and not a small group of white ones), Lena's name was sentimentally linked with that of the World Champion, but the small amount of gossip engendered was instigated because of the confusion regarding Lena's early marriage to Louis Jones.

Some enthusiastic, but uninformed reporter, thought he'd stumbled upon a "hot" item, but it soon petered out when it was discovered to be constructed much more out of fiction than of fact.

Lena's circumspect behavior, while encouraged originally by the studios and by Walter White of the N.A.A.C.P., was self-induced. She truly and quite simply does not like being around strangers. Usually her reactions don't take place in public, consequently the uproar her incident at the Luau, a Beverly Hills restaurant, created. And too, early in her career, Lena learned that one was particularly vulnerable it one was a celebrity.

Miss Calhoun sighs: "I can always remember poor Humphrey Bogart or Errol Flynn as targets for nightclub drunks. That's why I confine my social life to my family and a few friends. There is this constant pressure in public to live up to some sort of an 'image.' When in my lifetime I have been refused at a hotel, or turned down when I applied for an apartment, I would rather not have publicized it because it could and did happen to any black. But, on the other hand, because I am 'who I am' I could and can sometimes do more about it than the average black—and maybe help someone else along the way. I really hate the fact that my having been something 'special' made it possible for me to do more. But, if the end result justified the exposure, it has been a small price to pay."

In the roll-call of men who have been strong supports for Lena Calhoun Horne to lean upon, one cannot by pass Ralph Harris, her manager for more than thirty years. Harris, a white man, was a publisher of music in New York when his path crossed Lena's and Lennie's.

After Lennie's death, Lena come to depend more and more upon Ralph Harris and his judgement. It was Ralph Harris who produced the first Lena Horne special in England, "Lena," when American TV had evidenced no interest in the project.

Miss Calhoun grins wickedly, "Don't ask me why it took so long for domestic TV to cotton to black specials. Even Harry Belafonte's original specials came through the BBC." She winks one of her large eyes. "Both you and I know damned well why."

But it was Ralph Harris who took the bull by the horn and put "Lena" on the waves. Jon Scoffield directed the original show. Lena's singing was accompanied by the Jack Parnell orchestra with Lennie Hayton conducting. It was a good time for all.

When one looks at Lena Calhoun Horne, chanteuse celebre, ageless, with a svelte and suave body and face, one cannot help but ask the question, "What of marriage?"

Does Miss Calhoun in her solitude ever get lonely, ever feel the need for male companionship—especially since the deaths of Lennie, her father, and her son—the three men, not including Ralph Harris who were closest to her and were most involved in her career and her personal life.

Marriage?

Miss Calhoun shakes her pretty head and rolls her Modigliani neck in the turtleneck sweater.

"Marriage, I don't know. Honestly, I don't know. I'm pretty shy about male-female relationships. I like older men and the men I'm attracted to want younger women.

She looks at her favorite picture of Lennie and flashes that famous Horne smile. "You see Lennie and I had the one thing most marriages lack...mutual respect."

Miss Calhoun's watery eyes are as vocal as her singing. "I'm gonna love you, come rain or come shine..."

The photograph on page 192 may or may not be Miss Calhoun's favorite of Lena Horne but this casual, dressed-in-jeans, conversing over dinner candid is the author's favorite photograph of the beautiful Miss Calhoun.

CHAPTER TEN
"Just Me!"

In the house in Santa Barbara where Lena
Horne has set about creating a home for herself,
a home where she can be "Just me!" one
cannot help but be conscious of the fact that
this woman is essentially a product of a
"matriarchial culture."

In this identity with society Lena Horne is
not unique, because the history of the black
in America is the history of matriarchial society
created and fostered by the white by the white
man—from the day the slave owners first
brought the African to America's shores to

the present day of economic slavery which has in many instances reduced the black man from a "provider" to a welfare recipient. Certainly Lena's son, Teddy, working in Watts, saw the demoralizing results of the emasculation of the black male. When Lena became a part actively of the Black Revolution, she also became incorporated into the other contemporary social revolution of women's rights.

Miss Calhoun is extremely proud of her maternal and paternal grandmothers. She recognizes the fact that they were superior human beings in an era when most women were subservient to male demands. She also is aware that black women had for many years in America been the pivot around which the black family survived. The man's usefulness lay in his physical strength, the woman's in her child-bearing and child-rearing abilities. In the South, where most of the black women slaves lived, they were subjected to the physical advances not only of their black mates, but also the unwanted advances of their white owners. The black husband was forced under slave laws to accept the white man's child as his without complaint. In many instances his resentment found its outlet on the only living humans he could strike back at—his wife and his illegitimate children. Before and after the Civil War white children were often raised—in many instances even breast fed—by a black wet nurse when the white mother lacked sufficient milk. The black woman ran the household, especially in the homes of the rich and her word was law.

After the Civil War, when blacks moved North, it was most often the black woman who could find full-time employment as a domestic in the homes of white people. So, early in the history of the American black, we find the child looking to the mother for all of the needs of life and because this was the case in the majority of black families, a black matriarchial society emerged.

That Miss Calhoun's female ancestors were matriarchs no one would deny. But, the interesting fact is both her grandmothers were married to intelligent, hard working "profesional" men who sustained the male role and inculcated into young Lena the proper role of a man in a proper American middle-class family, white or black. It was not until the fallacies of such a structure became evident did the real revolt begin—for both blacks and for women, white and black.

The name Mary Wollstonecraft, may or my not have meant anything to Lena's grandmothers, but the contents of her manuscript *Vindication Of The Rights Of Women,* written in 1792, the original feminist manifesto, had left its mark. Mary wrote her book at a time when women, having about the same civil status as American slaves, were given superficial educations aimed at making them useful and pleasing to men. Wollstonecraft advocated providing them with serious education. She ascribed women's "follies" to "the natural effects of ignorance." Although she did not question the traditional belief that women belonged inside the home, she urged opening new areas of employment to them so they need never be driven to marry for economic reasons. She, at that time, had no conception of organizing women to gain concessions which men could not be persuaded to grant.

In 1848, the same year Alexander Stewart opened the first department store, Marble Dry Goods Palace on Broadway in New York, he opened without knowing a field of employment and enterprise for women and today for blacks. The Women's Rights Convention, the first in the world history, was held in Seneca Falls, New York. The three-hundred women conventioneers drew up the Seneca Falls Declaration, which propounded female equality with woman's suffrage. In the keynote address, Lucretitia Mott declared, "Man cannot fulfill his destiny alone, he cannot redeem his race unaided.... The world has never yet seen a truly great and virtuous nation, because in the degregation of women the very fountains of life are poisoned at their source.''

In the 1900s a young English woman, Marie Stopes, set forth the clarion call for the feminist stance in her book, *Married Love*. Marie Stopes believed that women should be equal partners with men, and wrote: ''When woman naturally develops the powers latent within her, man will find at his side, not only a mate, free and strong, but a desirable friend and intellectual companion.''

The women antecedents of Lena Horne knew the true meanings of these revolutionary, feminist words and Cora Calhoun Horne was an activist in promulgating their truths. Lena herself acknowleges the fact that, ''Black women have always been liberated—of necessity.''

Behind her words is the experience which gives meaning to Helen Reddy's lyrics, ''I Am Woman.'' For Lena Calhoun Horne is woman in the final sense of the word.

The life of Lena Calhoun Horne, although very private, is nevertheless an open book and it is a book which is the story of a remarkable woman, a woman of strength and conviction, a woman who has always been a lover of men. Never in her career did Lena call upon the press to come to her aid, to defend her. She has never had to. Her actions have always spoken louder than her words.

It was, in fact, a writer who first appealed to Lena to take an active stand in black politics—long before James Baldwin persuaded her to come to the Kennedy meeting. It was the deceased Louis Lomax, author of *To Kill A Black Man*, *The Reluctant African* and *The Negro Revolt*. Lomax, who was highly intelligent and extremely articulate, persuaded the shy, crowd-wary Lena Horne to step forth and speak as a concerned black artist. He knew the incredible number of listeners her words would command. She spoke before a CORE rally. She spoke with restraint holding back the deep venom that seethed in her blood and made her when she was alone with her friends spit forth her vitriol which embraces language far removed from the polished French and the properly spoken English she has at her command.

Once when Lena was touring with the The Basie Band, Al Collins, the disc jockey, introduced her: "And now, Ladies and Gentlemen, the next President of the United States, Miss Lena Horne."

Miss Calhoun laughs at the memory: "I'm politically aware, but you know what happens. They find something wrong about you—anything true or false—and make a big scandal and you're finished. You're running away before you really start running. Besides, today, I'm through proving anything. I just want to be me.''

Part of ''being me'' means being the mother of her daughter and the grandmother of Gail's two daughters. For a lady with a true matriarchal heritage that is no small task. There's a big, wide unsettled world out there for her progeny to try to live in.

There is no future Lena can predict, any more than can any other individual entering the decade of the 1990s.

''Being just me'' entails Miss Calhoun's natural love of home and home-making. Born under the sign of Cancer (a sign noted for love of home and family possessions) it is startling for a reader of astrology to see how well she survivied in the role of a ''gypsy,'' for most of her life has been spent as a wandering minstrel. Like most persons born under the sign of Cancer, Miss Calhoun likes food. When not doing the cooking herself, she is a ''gourmet''—a special lover of Creole delicacies such as gumbo. In fact, Miss Calhoun has a real taste for anything involving lobster. Once an admirer from New England flew a huge crate of live lobsters to her. She picked on lobster out of the crate and examined it closely and said; ''Man, that cat's dead.'' But when she examined it more closely and saw that the dark shelled creature wiggled and moved visibly, she shrieked, "Uh-huh! Playing possum, eh? Well in you go, brother!"

She turned to the reporter who was interviewing her and said, "You know that lobster had intelligence. Bet he tastes better than all the others."

But almost any lobster tastes good to Miss Calhoun, in addition to a good tender steak, baked potatoes or a fine bowl of chili. These are always tempting to the palate of Lena Horne.

Customarily, like most performers, Lena Horne dines after her performance. Like most performers, she has a queazy stomach before stepping on stage. Her only indulgence is a single martini mixed only by her friend and manager, Ralph Harris, who knows the exact proportion of ingredients to put together to relax her vocal chords and terminate the churning in her flat stomach.

Being "just me" also includes the theatrical career of Lena Calhoun Horne. There is a lot of competition out there today—Diana Ross, Dionne Warwick, Roberta Flack, Barbara Streisand—but there have always been a lot of "gal singers" out there. Still Lena Horne continues to be big box-office whenever she makes an appearance. She admits she would like to introduce songs of new singers, but her public demands the old familiar Lena Horne songs, Lena obliges but Miss Calhoun manages to slip an unfamiliar number into her repertoire. It's part of the Horne rebellion which is just as dynamic today as it ever was.

And finally, being "just me" means that peace which Lena Calhoun Horne associates with the story book house hidden from the human eye in Santa Barbara. It means the freedom to walk alone by the seashore, to listen to the song of the ocean, to let her thoughts wander into her past, her present and her future. Perhaps when she walks alone in her solitude her listening ear hears the voices and words of those with whom she has lived and loved.

Whatever the sounds and words, whether they be of love, of struggle, of wisdom, of hope, they are a chorus of a life that never ceases— the life of the artist.

The evening sun is setting as Miss Calhoun heads toward her home. Fog will soon embrace her figure as she vanishes from sight— temporarily—but anyone choosing to listen can hear the song on her lips:

"Stormy weather...since my man and I ain't together...keeps raining all the time."

The super star is finally at home. Will she continue with an active career and just dabble in music or vice-versa?

Miss Calhoun laughs as she closes the door.

"Honey—the stormy weather isn't over yet, so I'll continue to dabble in music so long as it activates the name of Lena Horne for other purposes."

She holds up her American Express Card and from her throat comes, "If you believe..."

As she said, she didn't sing it that sweet...even when she was playing Glinda, the Good Witch of the North.

The lights dim in the story book house and Miss Calhoun puts Lena Horne to rest between the pages of her life story.

A few months later Lena was back performing; a May, 1980 benefit for the Duke Ellington School of Arts held at the Kennedy Center in Washington, D.C. She got four standing ovations and said to an old friend, "Hell, I'm too young to retire from this."

A year later, on March 12, 1981, Miss Calhoun put Lena Horne to work again, seriously, when "Lena Horne, The Lady and Her Music" opened as a triumphant retrospective of her career. The musical sequences started with her early days at the Cotton Club and took her through her MGM days and her days as a singing American legend.

The show was a tour de force earned her the entertainment industry's top awards—the Drama Desk Award, the Antoinette Perry

(Tony) Award, the Handel Medallion, the Actors Equity Paul Robeson Award, The Dance Theater of Harlem's Emergence Award, and two Grammy Awards. Then she was awarded the N.A.A.C.P.'s highest honor, the Spingarn Medal. The Kennedy Center honored her for a lifetime of achievement in the performing arts.

"Lena Horne: The Lady and Her Music" closed in New York on June 30, 1982. It was Miss Calhoun's sixty-fifth birthday. She then took the show on an international tour, ending it two years later.

"I was tired and I needed family around me," she has said. Soon afterwards she moved to Washington, D.C. to be near daughter Gail and her grandchildren.

Still she performs now and then, mostly for charity causes. And picks up awards for her lifetime of achievements. And is again and again honorned as a true American legend.

PICTURE CREDITS

BRETT HOWARD was born in New York City and reared in Memphis, Tennessee, where her family was engaged in banking. A graduate of Smith College, she was a book editor in New York before turning to writing. Besides writing books on medical subjects with several well-known doctors, her short stories and articles have appeared in such magazines as The New Yorker, Esquire, The Los Angeles Magazine and CAD. Among her novels are *The Baroness of Harlem* and *Memphis Blues*. She is currently living in Los Angeles and writing a social history of Memphis similiar to her highly acclaimed *Boston, A Social History*.

INDEX

214

215

216

217

221

222